Enneagram Relationships

Comprehensive Beginner's Guide to Learn the
Realms of Enneagram

(A Journey to Discover Your Unique Path for
Spiritual Growth)

Christopher Joseph

Published by Knowledge Icons

Christopher Joseph

Enneagram Relationships: Comprehensive Beginner's Guide to Learn the Realms of Enneagram (A Journey to Discover Your Unique Path for Spiritual Growth)

ISBN 978-1-990084-53-9

Legal & Disclaimer

The information contained in this book is not designed to replace or take the place of any form of medicine or professional medical advice. The information in this book has been provided for educational and entertainment purposes only.

The information contained in this book has been compiled from sources deemed reliable, and it is accurate to the best of the Author's knowledge; however, the Author cannot guarantee its accuracy and validity and cannot be held liable for any errors or omissions. Changes are periodically made to this book. You must consult your doctor or get professional medical advice before using any of the suggested remedies, techniques, or information in this book.

Upon using the information contained in this book, you agree to hold harmless the Author from and against any damages, costs, and expenses, including any legal fees potentially resulting from the application of any of the information provided by this guide. This disclaimer applies to any damages or injury caused by the use and application, whether directly or indirectly, of any advice or information presented, whether for breach of contract, tort, negligence, personal injury, criminal intent, or under any other cause of action.

You agree to accept all risks of using the information presented inside this book. You need to consult a professional medical practitioner in order to ensure you are both able and healthy enough to participate in this program.

Table of Contents

Introduction

Hi there! Have you ever heard of the term; "Enneagram?" If you have, then congratulations. Getting to know about it is the first step, but applying it is the second and bold step. If you haven't, then it's no big deal. As a matter of fact, I was once in that position too. There were times I would even find myself in places I didn't even know I was; in a state, I could never have imagined myself in, a situation where I didn't understand the people around me. Trust me; it's not a good place to be.

But thanks to Enneagram, I was able to move past every hurdle and obstacle that had sworn to make my life miserable. I was ready to go into a fantastic state of understanding myself. With the understanding of the nine personality traits, I have been able to interact, mingle, and understand anybody that crosses my path; no matter how complicated some people appear to be. That is what Enneagram teaches you. Don't be surprised, it's all real, and it is precisely what I'm going to show you in the course of this book.

Now, don't get it twisted, Enneagram is no joke, neither is it something hard to pull off as many people had painted it over the past few years. It is, in fact, one of the simplest types of personality trait that you can study within the shortest time. Enneagram would give you a sound understanding of who you are, what your personality is, and a comprehensive understanding of the people around you.

In the words of Williams Shakespeare, I quote;

"If you don't understand yourself, nobody will understand you."

Be that as it may, Enneagram is the study of the nine personalities of people that shows you exactly how the human mind works and how various people react in different situations. You also need to know that understanding people also helps you determine your personality. This is because there is a high probability that the people whom you intend studying might also be studying you in return. Thus, the need for a complete understanding of Enneagram.

As a beginner in this field, it is essential to know that the relationships you have in society helps determine who you are. What happens then if you don't know anything about the society you live in? Your relationship with people will not turn out well and most likely not stand the test of time. While Enneagram is primarily used for understanding other people, it also gives a hint of who you are. It is pertinent to know that life situations go beyond personal dealings. If you have some knowledge about the personality of the people around you then relating with them on a more genuine level will undoubtedly be very easy. In other words, equating and understanding the nine personalities of people are the fundamental goals of this book.

There have been many books on Enneagram, but none of them could have combined the basic understanding of the concept with the in-depth knowledge in such a way that the beginners of Enneagram won't find the idea too difficult to handle. This is why the language used in this book is conversational and straightforward. Enneagram is not a complex phenomenon; it is a natural attribute that everyone possesses. Learning about our own personality helps in different ways. We can all enjoy who we are and our personality traits even better once we discover ourselves.

This book will serve as a simple guide for everyone on the Enneagram. Regardless of whether you are an expert or new to the concept, this book is meant for you. As an expert, you must have been familiar with this concept before now. However, there are lots of various insights that this book will expose you to, that you might not have heard of before. This book is designed to broaden your horizon and make you see beyond your level of imagination. On the other hand, as a beginner, it would build you up from scratch till you become an expert of your own in Enneagram.

As you go through the book, prepare to delve into the origin of the Enneagram, and then read on to learn about the latest research. The necessity of this is that you would be able to understand why and how Enneagram came into being and therefore, be confident in applying the knowledge, in your everyday life. It is also very paramount to know that social relations and behaviors of people cannot be guessed or given a thumbnail rule, but the underlying or causal factors could be understood. In short, you will learn, in the simplest way, underlying factors that impact the way people react to you and of course, how to deal with them appropriately.

Have you ever spoken to someone, and the reaction was different from what you expected? Have you ever noticed how different people would react in different situations? Do you think these are all just serendipity of behaviors? Understanding these strange behaviors is the goal of this book.

This is a book that combines personalities and their instincts. Many people have been waiting for a book that has these combinations even though there had been lots of books written in the past to fit one or the other. Now, the good news we bring is this - you can now get both combinations in a single book – this book. The majority of books that have been written on the topic have focused on these two combinations had always been written on religious grounds and tenets.

In other words, the nine personalities and their instincts have only been discussed in the religious setting over the years, with less consideration for other relations. After all, you can't use one single occurrence, religion, to determine all other ones. Aside from this combination, the style of the nine personalities is dealt with to get every bit of how Enneagram could be seen. This is where instincts are explained in clear and straightforward terms. An overview of the personalities through the diagram is described. The diagram will explain each style and how they are related.

In this book, you will also learn the primary and subsidiary personality of people through the understanding of the neuroscience of Enneagram. While many psychologists believe that there are nine personalities of people, neuroscientists discussed that one could detect some play-in-group personalities. In other words, the personalities of people, according to the neuroscience of Enneagram, are made up of two different components: the primary and secondary personality traits. We will go through all of that will throughout this book.

Additionally, as a parent or potential parent, you will learn how to handle your children with an understanding of their personalities. Of course, not everyone is a parent. However, everyone has had to deal with situations where these lessons can be applied. There is no denying that parenting is a complicated thing to do; however, when you understand it from the angle of the people's personalities, it becomes easier. This book will provide you every bit of this understanding.

Many people wonder why and how Enneagram applies to them. This is because many books have focused primarily on other people: this is a different book. You will learn how to apply these personalities to not only you but other situations around you as well. You will be taken through a personality test. This test will be used to ascertain the personalities of the people around you, and that would be within the shortest possible time. Instead of following other methods that would waste your precious time and end up eating through your timeline, Enneagram would save you from time-wasting; it is fast, reliable, and perfect.

You can see this new skill (knowing the personality of people within the shortest time) as a detective trait in you. You now possess the power to see through people, to understand the emotions & personalities of people, and to make use of the nine personality traits to your advantage. One last thing you need to know before we start this journey together, do not misuse the knowledge you will gain from this book. Being selfless is of the essence when reading people's personality. When we help people become a better version of what they were yesterday by reading through their personality, then we are doing a good thing. But using those same powers to manipulate anyone is merely unacceptable.

It is important to remember that this book has been constructed to give you an introduction to what Enneagram is all about. This is why it is for everyone. Its ultimate goal is to familiarize you with the knowledge of the concept of Enneagram in the simplest way. While going about that dream job, have you ever wondered who will be conducting the interview? What they're like? What makes them tick? Well, the trick is in this book. Now, let's get to it, shall we?

Chapter 1: What Is Enneagram: Definition

The Enneagram may be a system of temperament writing that describes patterns in however folks create by mental act the planet and manage their emotions. The Enneagram model describes 9 completely different temperament types and maps every of those types on a nine-pointed diagram that helps for instance however the kinds relate to 1 another. The name Enneagram comes from the Greek: Ennea is that the Greek word for 9 and grass suggests that one thing that's drawn or written.

According to the Enneagram, each temperament encompasses a sure perspective and appears at the planet through theirown lens or filter. This makes it attainable to clarify why folks behave in sure ways that. By describing however the essential temperament adapts and responds to each nerve-racking and corroborative things, the Enneagram shows opportunities for private development and provides a foundation for the understanding of others.

The system has been the inspiration for multiple Enneagram temperament tests also as books on an eclectic style of subjects, from personal development and religious growth, to relationships and even career development.

The Peacemaker
9
The Challenger 8 — 1 The Reformer
The Enthusiast 7 — 2 The Helper
The Loyalist 6 — 3 The Achiever
The Investigator 5 — 4 The Individualist

Enneagram with its 9 types

Understanding The Enneagram Image

The basis of the Enneagram may be a nine-pointed geometric image. It consists of an outer circle, on that the 9 points (personalities) are numbered right-handed and equally spaced. There's additionally a triangle between the points nine, three and half-dozen and an irregular polygonal shape that connects the opposite points. The circle represents the wholeness and unity of human life whereas the opposite shapes represent however it's divided.

The kinds on either aspect of every core type are known as wings. The Enneagram doesn't create any sudden jumps between the 9 kinds, and few individuals are utterly and completely one kind. One or each the wings could influence our ways that of thinking and acting and are integrated into someone's overall temperament.

Each basic kind within the Enneagram is also connected by two lines to 2 different basic types; as an example, kind one is connected to kind seven and kind four. The primary line connects to the kind that the person has left behind or pent-up in childhood; the characteristics of this kind should be reintegrated so as for the person to develop. The second line connects to the kind that the person could grow into once they're able to reach the next stage of development.

These connecting lines highlight however every basic kind possesses indispensable strengths; however at a similar time have darker sides that are jam-packed with challenges. The inclusion of those lines moves the Enneagram from a strictly descriptive temperament model to at least one that's dynamic.

History

The word Enneagram comes from the Greek words ennea ("nine") and gram. The 9 completely different Enneagram kinds, known as numbers One through 9, mirror distinct habits of thinking, feeling, and behaving, with every kind connected to a novel path of development. Every folks has just one place, or number, on the Enneagram; whereas our Enneagram kind remains a similar throughout our period of time, the characteristics of our kind could either soften or become a lot of pronounced as we tend to grow and develop. Additionally to our core Enneagram kind, there are four different kinds that give further qualities to our personalities; these are known as wings and arrows.

The Enneagram's actual ancient history is unsure, though the system 1st appeared in each Asia and therefore the Mideast many thousand years ago or longer. As a result of it evolved as an oral tradition, it's tough to grasp its precise origins. Over time, the Enneagram has emerged in varied components of the planet, and its fashionable usage has been heavily influenced by 3 people. 2 philosophers began operating with the Enneagram on completely different continents: G.I. Gurdjieff within the Thirties in Europe, and accolade Ichazo from the 1950s to the current in South America. Claudio Naranjo, and yank medical specialist born in Chile, at first studied the Enneagram with Ichazo and brought it to us the 1970s.

The modern use of the Enneagram has adult from the work of those 3 people and has been advanced by different academics, among them Helen of Troy golf player, Don Riso, David Daniels, Russ Hudson, Theodorre Donson, Kathy Hurley, Tom Condon, and Hun Wagner. Sadly, Don Riso and Theodorre Donson aren't any longer alive, however their dedication and work continues to the touch several lives. Thousands of Enneagram books are currently in print everywhere the planet, as well as some translations of major Enneagram academics and others written by a rising cluster of latest Enneagram authors and teachers.

Where Did The Enneagram Return From?

It was left to a different person, Oscar Ichazo, to attach the Enneagram to temperament. Ichazo claimed to own discovered the temperament kind which means of the Enneagram once it absolutely was educated to him by the Archangel Metraton whereas he was high on psychedelic drug.

One of Ichazo's students, a Chilean-born head-shrinker named Claudio Naranjo (another occultist) was the primary to attach the 9 points of the Enneagram to 9 basic temperament varieties. (Naranjo additionally seems to be the one to attach the mention of the Enneagram by Gurdjieff and Ouspensky to ancient sources.)

In the Seventies, students of Naranjo unfold the Enneagram to numerous Catholic communities, particularly in mystical and contemplative circles. A number of the promoters of the Enneagram embrace the previous Jesuit Don Riso, the Franciscan religious Richard Rohr, and late Benedictine nun Suzanne Zuercher.

In 1997, Riso co-founded the Enneagram Institute, a company that helped bring the Enneagram to a broader audience.

Should Christians Be Victimization The Enneagram?

While the Enneagram is itself not ancient, typological temperament classifications are around since the age once book was reconstruction the walls of capital of Israel.

During that amount the Greek Dr. Medical practitioner was advancing his proto-psychological theory regarding the "four temperaments." The "father of medicine" known four elementary temperament types—sanguine, choleric, melancholic, and unemotional—that he believed were influenced by the four humors—blood, phlegm, and humor.

While doctors now not attribute our temperament to our bodily fluids, the thought that our personalities are often mapped to basic classes has lived on. Throughout the ages, Christians have fastened on to such typologies, therefore it's not stunning evangelicals would be interested in the newest variation.

Still, it raises the queries of whether or not we must always be anxious due to the Enneagram's person origins.

We positively should be anxious once the Enneagram is getting used, as several Catholics have, as a diversity of Gnostic-based subject area. We tend to shouldn't be seeking divination from a tool that was developed by somebody who claims it absolutely was bimanual to him in a vastly vision from what sounds suspiciously kind of a demon.

When the Enneagram is employed merely as a diagnostic tool or for temperament classification, the question decreases clear. Despite its origin story, there is also enough of the Enneagram that continue to be helpful (or a minimum of non-harmful).

However, we must always be continuing with caution and treat the problem like Paul treated meat sacrificed to idols (Rom. 14:14-23) if victimization the Enneagram causes our "weaker brothers" to stumble. If they start to assume New Age-oriented tools of "self-discovery" also are legitimate, we must always be willing to abandon the Enneagram altogether.

"But it's been, from its origin (whenever that was), infused with non secular significance. And in that lies the danger."

Evangelicals involved regarding the Enneagram ought to in all chance worry less, since it's probably a principally harmless fashion that may dissolve in a very few years. And evangelicals enthralled with the Enneagram ought to in all probability surprise why they're outlay such a lot of energy on a tool that has regarding the maximum amount of scientific validity because the four humors theory of medical practitioner.

Enneagram Figures

An Enneagram could be a nine-pointed two-dimensional figure. It's generally referred to as a nonagram or nonangle.

The name Enneagram combines the numeral prefix, ennea-, with the Greek suffix -gram. The -gram suffix derives from γραμμῆς (grammēs) that means a line

Regular Enneagram

A regular Enneagram (a nine-sided star polygon) is built victimization identical points because the regular enneagon however connected in fastened steps. It's 2 forms, described by a Schläfli image as and , connecting every second and each fourth points severally.

There is conjointly a star figure, or 3, made up of the regular enneagon points however connected as a compound of 3 equal triangles. (If the triangles are alternately latticed, this leads to a Brunnian link.) This star figure is usually called the star of Goliath, when or 2, the Star of David

Compound

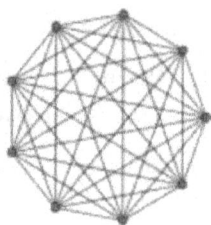

Regular star

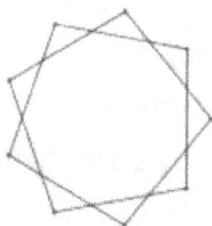

Regular compound

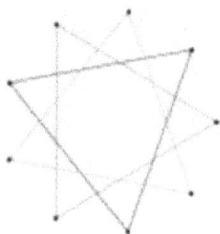

Regular star

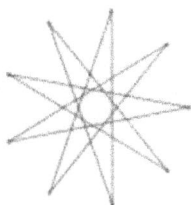

Other Enneagram figures

The Bahá'í nine-pointed star

The ultimate stellation of the polyhedron has 2-isogonal Enneagram faces. It's a 9/4 wound star solid. The Fourth Way teachings and therefore the Enneagram of temperament use an irregular Enneagram consisting of a triangle and an irregular.

Chapter 2: How To Know Your Enneagram

Number

The Enneagram is a system that can be used to identify your personality type. It is based on a circle that has nine points along its edge. Each of those nine points represents a separate, distinct personality.

"The Enneagram system describes these nine broad personality types or archetypes: the Perfectionist, the Helper, the Achiever, the Romantic, the Observer, the Questioner, the Adventurer, the Asserter, and the Peace Seeker."-Elizabeth Wagele

Wings and Arrows

In addition to that personality type, represented by a number, we each are influenced by the numbers next to ours. These are called wings. And we have influence as well, from our arrows, which are lines drawn from our number to two others on the edge of the Enneagram circle.

Subtypes

In Enneagram theory, each personality type has three subtypes based on three of our basic instincts: self-preservation, relationships and social needs. Each person operates within those subtypes in a style that reflects that particular type. But usually, we will lean more heavily on one of them than the others.

Self-Preservation: this subtype focuses on being self-sufficient and may put a lot of energy and attention into their homes.

Relational: this subtype focuses on making connections and can be energetic and intense.

Social: this subtype either draws energy from being part of a group or goes in the other direction and avoids social contact.

Learning about the Enneagram

The first purpose of learning about the Enneagram personality system is to understand yourself better. The second is to respect and appreciate the differences in yourself and those who are represented by another number. There is no personality type that is better than any other.

Each one has great qualities and each one has ways of thinking and behaving, motivations, that cause discomfort and pain. Growth and healing, a third purpose of learning about the Enneagram, involves increasing or maximizing the use of the strengths in your personality type, your wing and your arrows, and healing the weaknesses in these areas.

The Enneagram can be used to help you understand who you are at the core, help you improve your relationships with others and help you identify jobs and careers you would be suited to based on your Enneagram personality type.

One of the big considerations in the study of the modern Enneagram is mis-typing. You probably know someone who typed themselves based on a book or website and you might not agree with that they decided. And, as hard as this is to hear, many of us type ourselves based on who we hope or think we are instead of how we really are.

This Guide is meant to help you affirm your type, or help you discover your type for the first time while avoiding the common pitfalls that come with self-typing.

Without further ado, here are the...

7 Things to Consider When Finding (or Affirming) Your Type:

1. Make sure you have a basic understanding of each type before you delve into typing yourself.

Just like you need to know the premise of how a re car works before deciding if it's the brakes or the radiator, you have to have an understanding of the nine types before you can know with certainty of your own type. I would suggest looking at http://www.EnneagramBook.com to get a feel for each type. While you are browsing, make sure to note any types that you feel are REALLY you, or REALLY NOT you.

2. Take the free Enneagram Test.

There are a few tests out there that will attempt to find your type by an online test. Although these are far from infallible, they certainly are a part of the process. I won't recommend one in particular, but you can Google "Enneagram Test" to find one that suits your needs.

3. Answer the questions on the test honestly.

Make sure you don't answer the way you like to think of yourself, or want yourself to be! It's so easy to do this, but the value in the Enneagram is only available to you if you get your correct type. So make sure to be honest!

4. Remember that all types are equal.

Many times people hear they are a 4 and wonder if that is less than a 1 or half of an

8. The numbers are just symbols. All of the types are different, equal, interesting, beautiful, and have something to offer. Love your type!

5. Find your wing.

Each Enneagram type has a wing. Wings can make a huge difference in your type. Although not everyone agrees on the authenticity of the wing, I have found it to be true more of the time than false, so I still suggest it. Your wing can be one of the two numbers sequentially adjacent to your type number. For instance, a type three could have a wing of a 2 or a 4. It would be written like this 3w2 or 3w4. A type 6 could have a 5 wing or a 7 wing. See the pattern?

In order to find your wing, I would look at Enneagrambook.com under your type number and find the wing section and see which one seems to fit you more. The wings are typically much easier to decipher than your type.

6. Remember that you might not see your type so clearly in yourself.

It is very hard to see ourselves with objectivity. You might not see the parts of you the make up your Enneagram type immediately, that's why it is important to do step number 7...

7. Find a study group, student, or practitioner of the Enneagram to affirm your findings and help you take the next step.

Find a local Enneagram group that you can call or go to a meeting. It is very easy for someone to hang out with you for a couple hours and after having a few conversations let you know if you have found the right number. Someone's type is a lot about their "energy", and someone who has been practicing and studying the Enneagram for a while has honed their aim. Plus, a great many teachers think the "oral tradition" of the Enneagram is really the only way the lineage can be passed. So if you are truly interested, having a group of friends and a group to learn with and from is truly the most powerful tool you can have!

Finding your type is just the start in your path down this amazing tool called the Enneagram. Make sure you find the right type and you have done yourself a great favor. As always, live well, love lots, and keep growing.

Chapter 3: Historical Origins Of The

Enneagram

The Enneagram has a rich history, with its roots in several ancient traditions. It is one of the oldest human development systems in the world—parts of the sacred Enneagram tool date back thousands of years.

The exact path of the Enneagram is somewhat unclear. What most experts agree upon is that this theory, in some form, has existed for centuries. The philosophy behind the Enneagram likely has its roots in several different religions. There is some proof that it has connections to early Christianity, Judaism, and Islam and Buddhism.

Some believe the Enneagram's earliest roots can be traced back to Desert Fathers in Egypt. This group was known to have spread their wisdom over many centuries.

Others argue that the Enneagram was first established back in the days of Pythagorean mathematics hundreds of years ago. Pythagoreans have long been recognized as having a rich understanding and appreciation of numbers.

One additional theory is that a 4th-century philosopher named Evagrius Ponticus first described several concepts that have since been connected with Enneagram theory. Ponticus preached about eight deadly thoughts and the eight potential remedies to these thoughts. Some people believe that these conceptions influenced the development of the Enneagram as a personality tool.

Variations of the Enneagram symbol also appear in Islamic Sufi traditions, although at the time, the meaning might not have been the same. Sufis were known for passing down different forms of wisdom through many generations. There is some indication that in the 14th century, a Sufi group known as the "Brotherhood of the

Bees" may have communicated with others about this figure.

Contemporary ideas of the Enneagram seem to have derived for the most part from the teachings of Claudio Naranjo and Oscar Ichazo. The work of Naranjo and Ichazo has been traced back to the influence of George Gurdjieff (1870-1949).

Most experts agree that Gurdjieff was the individual who made the Enneagram figure widely known. Gurdjieff was a Russian philosopher and teacher who studied under Freud. He is said to have been first introduced to the Enneagram in the 1920s, and from that point on, used this symbol in his teachings. Gurdjieff relied on the Enneagram to help explain the unfolding of the universe. However, there is no evidence that he ever taught the Enneagram as a system for understanding or categorizing human personality. At one time Gurdjieff claimed that while in Afghanistan in the late 1800s, in a Sufi community, he came across the symbol of the Enneagram.

A man named Oscar Ichazo from Bolivia is recognized as the one who developed the nine personality types that are associated with the Enneagram. Ichazo was well known for teaching programs of self-development back in the 1950s and used the Enneagram figure within his work. He eventually formed a school in South America, and in the late 1960s, he began teaching the Enneagram as we know it today. Ichazo was the first to coin the term "Enneagram of Personality," and the first to correlate the nine points of the Enneagram to nine specific personality types.

Enneagram of Personality was part of a larger body of teaching that Ichazo referred to as "photo analysis." In his work, Ichazo focused on mapping out different personality traits and explaining how to use these traits for success.

Claudio Naranjo was a psychologist who learned about the Enneagram of Personality from Ichazo while working in Chile. Before too long, Naranjo began further developing this concept and bringing it to a more modern conception. He started teaching about Enneagram back in the early 1970s, elaborating on Ichazo's ideas about human personality. This system caught on with a group of Jesuits who brought the teachings to the United States. The Jesuits ended up adapting the Enneagram for use in Christian spirituality.

Additional influences on the origins of the Enneagram can be linked to Robert Ochs and Helen Palmer, who studied the Enneagram system under Naranjo in the early 1970s. Ochs did his part to introduce the Enneagram to various Christian communities and began to teach this system among Jesuit circles.

Throughout the 1980s and 1990s, many books were published on the Enneagram of Personality. Richard Rohr learned about the Enneagram from his own research and was the first to publish a book about Enneagram in the English language. With his book called "The Enneagram: A Christian Perspective," published in 1990, he was the first to bring this concept into the mainstream. Rohr's book increased interest in the Catholic community about this notion and explained how Christians might benefit from its teachings. Rohr identified the root sin of each type and the ways in which those sins could be redeemed. He also explained how the Enneagram could be used to transform lives and lead people to God. This was groundbreaking work on the Enneagram and tied this symbol to a broader spiritual, psychological spectrum. It was Rohr's work that turned the Enneagram into a conventional, widely used personality tool.

Contemporary History

The Enneagram brings together ancient beliefs and modern psychology. Some people may be surprised to learn that Enneagram has had only about 70-80 years of application in its modern form. Teachings of this instrument continue to gain in popularity across the globe. As knowledge about this tool continues to grow, so does its influence on modern psychology.

Many people still use Gurdjieff's work today as a basis for teaching how the Enneagram can lead to personal transformation. They continue to explore and expand their application into mainstream culture. It is well recognized that human beings today have more and more of a desire for self-awareness, and the Enneagram is a great way to encourage this awareness.

Today many different psychologists, philosophers, and Enneagram experts teach this assessment tool via seminars, conferences, books, and video. Workshops on Enneagram of Personality are taught nearly everywhere around the world. This tool is used by psychologists, life coaches, and counselors for helping people learn more about themselves and their relationships. It is quickly becoming more and more popular as a simple but effective way of understanding one's personality and for increasing personal growth.

Using the Enneagram can also be helpful in understanding and improving interpersonal relationships in the workplace. This system is now widely promoted in the business world, and countless companies and agencies have relied on this tool as a way of improving teamwork and collaboration in the office.

Many scientific studies have set out to validate the basis of the Enneagram. The most common scientific validation of the Enneagram test is called the Riso-Hudson Enneagram Type Indicator (RHETI). This instrument was created in 2004 by Rebecca Newgent and is still the most widely accepted of its kind.

The number of people who self-discover with Enneagram continues to grow both in religious and non-religious circles. The beauty of this system is that you are likely to find it helpful despite your race, culture, worldview, religion, or status. There are no boundaries or limitations surrounding this tool. In fact, over time, the Enneagram has led to the integration of psychological knowledge about personalities with a more spiritual approach to being.

Sacred Christian Perspective

Although it likely dates back to pre-Christian times and sources, the Enneagram comes from a tradition of healing and is often interpreted through a Christian framework. Many people in today's culture choose to approach Enneagram from a biblical perspective, and it has been used for decades in Catholic retreats and seminars. Enneagram of personality is commonly referred to as a "sacred map to the soul." There is some proof that early references to Sacred

Enneagram have been found in the writings of a few very early Christian writers. These writings describe the important healing components of the human soul.

An important concept in the Christian faith is the belief that part of a good Christian's purpose in this world is to develop a deeper relationship with God. Many people believe that the nine personality types associated with Sacred Enneagram each have their own unique path to God. They believe this tool is not just about determining a personality type, but more importantly, it is meant to help people find one of the nine paths back to their true selves. Only by uncovering this path will someone truly find love and happiness.

Christians believe that there are many different ways of praying, studying, and worshipping that can help an individual on their journey to God. They believe that depending on life circumstances, not all of these ways may be completely fulfilling over the course of a lifetime. Sometimes, in order to get to a deeper relationship with God, one must find new, more powerful ways of connecting.

One suggestion for doing this is to return to some of the ways that are rooted in the old Christian tradition. Great Christian theologians talk about the importance of knowing your true, authentic self. It is widely understood that in order to know God, this step must first be completed. Christians believe that wisdom can guide you on your personal journey and that increasing your self-knowledge can make you feel more alive and more whole.

In Christianity, redemption from the false self is considered very important. God loves everyone unconditionally, even through weaknesses, faults, and darkness, but the closer you can be to your authentic self, the closer you can be to God. Gaining knowledge and insight into yourself will also increase your ability to trust your God-given gifts.

An Enneagram is a useful tool for helping you restore your heart and mind to your authentic self. It is often said to be a "mirror of the soul." The aim of this personality assessment is to understand better yourself, your deepest potential, and the possibilities that exist for you. Some believe the Enneagram to be a tool by which God shows you your blind spots and helps you overcome your weaknesses. It is a system that has the capacity to show you ways to heal your broken psyche.

Sacred Enneagram helps you discover what your personality type is, and what it might look like for you to enter into a deeper kind of spirituality. Although it does not align perfectly with Christian faith, discovering yourself through Enneagram can perhaps help you find a deeper and more authentic relationship with yourself, and with God. Keep in mind that the passage to self-improvement can be difficult; it requires courage to take this task on!

Chapter 4: Structure And Design

The Figure

The symbol of the Enneagram begins with a circle, a pure symbol of unity in many cultures that completes a cycle, a simple of wholeness, of being complete.

Added to the ring of the base circle, are 9 numbered points, equidistantly placed on the outer edge. Each of these points is numbered, starting with 9 at the top and moving downward in the count to the number one, going around the circle in a counterclockwise manner.

No number holds superiority to any other; they are only indicators. Just because 9 is at the top, it does not mean that this number is better than any other number around the circle. Each and every Enneatype holds value. You hold value.

If we were to divide this circle (without the inner lines as depicted above), we could separate it into 3, with a "Y" shape whose lines would fall between 1 and 2, 4 and 5, and 7 and 8. This creates 3 equal pieces of the whole circle, which become "Centers" of being for the personality types we are going to be delving into.

8, 9, and 1 form the top arc of the circle, whose personality types generally adhere to an Instinctive Center, whose predominant emotional reaction to the loss of connection with the self tends to be Anger or Rage.

2, 3, and 4 form the lower right arc of the circle, whose personality types generally adhere to a Feeling Center, whose predominant emotional reaction to the loss of connection with the self tends to be Shame.

5, 6, and 7 form the lower left arc of the circle, whose personality types generally adhere to a Thinking Center, whose predominant emotional reaction to the loss of connection with the self tends to be Fear.

This is not to say that any or all of these qualities and/or emotions are not present in any or all of the other parts of the circle. However, these personality types and the way they generally tend to operate in an average situation based on their proximity to one another give us a basis of understanding before we even get into the far deeper workings of the circle.

Inside the circle, each of these numbers is connected via lines placed simply. The first lines placed is an equilateral triangle, 3 lines, connecting points 9, 3, and 6. These are the middle points of our Centers, helping to define our ways of thought. The triangle itself is representative of the "Law of Three," which gives us a basis for looking into each Enneatype from a Heart (Feeling Center), Head (Thought Center), and Body (or Gut-Instinctive Center) approach.

The final lines, connecting points 1, 4, 2, 8, 5, and 7, form what is called a "periodic figure," which is an irregularly designed hexagonal shape. Known as the "Law of Seven," these lines symbolize the 7 deadly sins, those things or aspects of self that can prevent from moving into a higher state of being, and thus, must be worked on devoutly if we wish to progress in an upward fashion in our personal development and growth.

The Set-Up

The ultimate way in which the lines are set up within the Enneagram circle shows us who we are at our center point (which is determined through the taking and scoring of the Enneagram Test).

The first line coming from our Center point shows us where we go to on the circle in times of Stress, or unhealthy periods of our lives. These points are also sometimes referred to as Disintegration points.

The second line coming from our Center point shows where we go to in times of Growth when we feel Secure or during the healthier periods in our lives. These points are sometimes referred to as Integration points.

Obviously, there is more to it than that, but this is the easiest, most simplistic way of looking at and starting to understand what the Enneagram is, and how you can work with it for your personal growth and betterment.

The Types

And this brings us to the start of our discovering the actual personality types that are defined by the Enneagram theory. These will be listed below in sequential number order, for the sole purpose of listing each point, although, as stated above, they can actually be better defined as being described in groups of three, based on the initial Centers to which each fall under.

There are essentially nine types that define personalities under the Enneagram. While each has primary names that they are known by, they are also called other names under different forms of the Enneagram. Below you will find a list of each primary name, based on the characteristic role that defines their personality type, and some of the aliases that they are also known by

1 The Perfectionist, The Reformer

2 The Helper, The Giver

3 The Achiever, The Performer

4 The Individualist, The Romantic

5 The Investigator, The Observer

6 The Loyalist, The Loyal Skeptic

7 The Enthusiast, The Epicure

8 The Challenger, The Protector

9 The Peacemaker, The Mediator

These personality types are further refined by their subtypes, stressors, growth processes, the level of evolution on the ladder under each type, and so much more that we are about to go further into, starting with the basic equilateral triangle of Heart, Mind, and Body.

Chapter 5: The Perfectionist

The first type of personality is the perfectionist, also often called the reformer. Every personality type has a set of words which accurately describe the personality. While you will always want to read through your personality type description, you can also gain an idea of your personality through these few words. For the perfectionist, the descriptive words are perfectionistic, self-controlled, purposeful, and principled.

What is the Perfectionist

When people think of the word perfectionist, they automatically think of a person who is driven, controlling, and needs to make sure everything is always right. While all of this is true about this personality type, like with all other personalities, there are levels of integration. These levels give a range of how healthy or unhealthy a person's personality is. For example, someone with a perfectionist personality who is at an unhealthy level won't listen to someone who contradicts what he or she believes. However, if the type two personality is at a healthy level, then the perfectionist personality is tolerant, accepting, and understands that while he or she wants to be as perfect as possible, perfection is not possible to achieve ("Type One," n.d.).

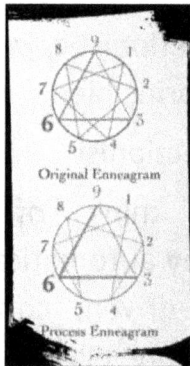

The true meaning of someone with a type one personality is that they have a very clear concept of what is right and wrong. They understand rules and ethics and think they should be followed thoroughly. At the same time, they want to see positive change and will do what they feel they need to do in order to make this change happen ("Type One," n.d.).

People with a type one personality have a strong fear of making mistakes. This is why they often take more time in completing a task. They need to make sure they are doing everything as perfectly as they can so mistakes will be limited. They often feel like everything needs to be in a certain order and can maintain high standards. Some of their flaws include not having patience, becoming too controlling, and resentful ("Type One," n.d.).

The perfectionists' biggest fear is corruption. While there are many reasons for this, one of the biggest is that they see corruption as unorderly and lacking control. When there is corruption, ethical standards are not followed and the conditions are not improving ("Type One," n.d.).

The biggest desire for a perfectionist is to be the best person possible. The perfectionist wants to be a good person overall, even if he or she exhibits personality traits of impatience and withdraws from other people. These traits are often used as a defense mechanism to help the type one manage their perfectionist traits. Type one also wants to see a well-balanced world around them.

Some people who are known to have type one personalities are Katherine Hepburn, Maggie Smith, Tina Fey, Hilary Clinton, Michelle Obama, Joan of Arc, Nelson Mandela, Jerry Seinfeld, Prince Charles, Jimmy Carter, and Kate Middleton ("Type One," n.d.).

People who have type one personality feel the need to have a mission to accomplish. Not only do they have a mission to focus on, but they will also do whatever they can to fulfill this mission. At the same time, they feel the need to justify their actions to themselves. They will do this by asking themselves questions to why this mission is important and conducting research. If they decide their actions are justified, they become very passionate and work hard to make improvements.

The type one personality won't often let themselves stray from their mission or responsibilities ("Type One," n.d.). Because of this, they can become resentful towards others or the conditions. This can often make the perfectionist seem controlling and unable to adapt to his or her surroundings. However, this is generally not true. The problem is because the perfectionist is struggling to improve conditions, they become frustrated and act out aggressively or become resentful. This is the way many type one personalities manage their struggles, mistakes, and the realization that the situation is uncontrollable.

Level of Integration

As stated earlier, all personalities have a level of integration. These consist of three different levels, which are healthy, average, and unhealthy. Within these levels are smaller levels which range from one to nine. The healthy level consists of levels one through three. The moderate level consists of levels four through six, and the unhealthy level consists of levels seven through nine. Level one means a type one personality at its best. Of course, the level will either increase or decrease depending on how the type one personality deals with his or her environmental situations. This means that when a personality reaches an unhealthy level, such as nine, he or she is at their worst.

Healthy Level

When a type one personality is at level one, they are performing at their best. They have found ways to manage their stress during situations that keeps them from becoming too aggressive and controlling. While they don't always manage everything perfectly, they realize that this is fine because perfection doesn't truly exist. However, this won't keep them from continuing to try. They also realize that they cannot control various environmental factors or what other people do. Therefore, they feel calmer when things don't go as planned. They think that as long as they perform their best, they are successful. They know that as long as they are mindful of the moment, they will be able to see and give others the truth (Cloete, n.d.).

Perfectionists at level two healthy level continue to work to improve themselves as they know they can be better. At this level, the type one will know what is right from wrong. Furthermore, they will understand ethics in all environments, from a working standpoint to religious ethics. They remain strong when it comes to their own moral values and strive to become self-disciplined. They are also very responsible, mature, and rational about circumstances ("Type One," n.d.).

A level three type one is at a lower healthy level. They still maintain a healthy way of keeping their aggression controlled in most situations. They strive to continue to do their best. They are rational and very concerned about ethics and making sure they are followed. These levels tend to make great teachers because of the belief that they have a higher purpose to make sure others see the truth. They also believe in fairness, even within state and federal laws ("Type One," n.d.).

Average Level

The highest level for a type one under the average level is a level four. People who are at this level can't always control their behaviors over their emotions. They believe that it is up to them to improve society's conditions, which is a belief they are very passionate about. Unlike the perfectionists at a healthy level, they don't always think rationally about their actions and can sometimes find themselves resentful or aggressive. This usually is shown through telling people that what they are doing is wrong and explaining how things should be instead (Cloete, n.d.).

A perfectionist, who is at a level five, is often considered a "workaholic." They strive to make sure everything has an order, including their emotions. While they do tend to become overly emotional, especially when they make mistakes, they do their best to keep these emotions hidden from other people. Like most perfectionists, they are known to have a strong sense of what is right and wrong, however, they can also be impressionable. This can cause them to follow people who won't help them achieve their order and in turn they will make mistakes. When this happens, the type one can become resentful (Cloete, n.d.).

A level six perfectionist has strong opinions and is highly critical of other people and themselves. Type one personalities at the lowest average level don't watch their reactions as well as other perfectionists do. Therefore, they are often deemed to be angry and impatient. Furthermore, they are known to scold people who they believe are doing wrong. These perfectionists like to have things done their way and don't believe that any other way is correct (Cloete, n.d.).

Unhealthy Level

An unhealthy level for a type one personality is a level seven. People who are in this category are often referred to as bullies. They are people who believe that no one else is right, except for them. In fact, some people refer to perfectionists at this level as narcissists. They can become very angry and lack patience when things aren't as they should be ("Type One," n.d.).

A level eight perfectionist often becomes so focused on what wrong things other people are doing that they lose track of what wrong things they are doing themselves. When this happens, they can find themselves doing the opposite of what they think is right. They tend to be very illogical thinkers and can have trouble problem-solving as they tend to do what they feel is right instead of what is actually right. They don't have a clear sense of morals and values as much as other type one personalities above them do ("Type One," n.d.).

A level nine represents a type one being at their lowest level of integration. They struggle in several areas for various reasons. Some perfectionists at this level are diagnosed with various mental illnesses, such as severe depression and obsessive-compulsive disorder. Unfortunately, suicidal thoughts and suicide are also high at this level (Cloete, n.d.).

Subtypes of the Perfectionist

Social Category is Non-Adaptable

Perfectionists are non-adaptable because they follow the rules and morals of what is right. They also believe that it is their job to make things right, if they see them as wrong, and are not typically flexible in this area. One of their biggest motivations to make things right is to make sure there is fairness (Cloete, n.d.).

Self-Preservation Category is Worry

Perfectionists spend a lot of time worrying because they want to make sure everything they do and everything that is around them is right. Therefore, they not only worry about their actions but the actions of others. This can cause them to feel anxious, especially when they believe that things aren't going as planned. Part of this is because they need to make sure they are well-prepared for their current situations. This not only includes making sure everything is in an orderly fashion, but also noticing every single detail which other people may miss (Cloete, n.d.).

One-on-One Category is Zeal

Zeal is known as a countertype. Depending on the healthy, average, and unhealthy level of a type one personality, it will determine how well they manage their personal relationships. Because many believe they are right, they feel authorized to tell others they are wrong. This can often cause all sorts of conflict when it comes to close relationships (Cloete, n.d.).

Relationships with Other Types

Type one is compatible with every other personality type. No matter what type they come in contact with, they can work with the individual. Of course, each personality will bring its own positivity and challenges to the relationship. For example, when it comes to a type one working with another type one, they will often run into conflict because they both strongly believe that they know only one of them is right. Therefore, if they don't agree on something, they will struggle to find any type of happy-medium. Perfectionists are very compatible with types nine, two, five, seven, and eight. They will struggle more with types one, three, four, and six. However, all this will also depend on the level of integration a type one associates with, along with the level of integration the other personality type associates with ("Relationships (Type Combinations)," n.d.).

Wing Types

The two wing personalities for the perfectionist are type nine and type two. Both of these wings will give the perfectionist positives and challenges. The positives for type nine are their drive, helping perfectionists become more relaxed, becoming more considerate of other people, and understanding that other people can also be right. One of the challenges that type nine brings to type one is that they might neglect situations which are difficult and in turn self-neglect.

The positives which type two brings to the perfectionist are taking care of themselves, helping others, and having compassion for other people. The challenges type two can bring to type one are the feeling of being taken advantage of and becoming overly sensitive to what other people think about them (Cloete, n.d.).

Center Point

A type one personality falls under the body center (Cloete, n.d.). If you have a type one personality, you will internalize your anger. People who have type one personality are very self-critical and often hard on themselves to a fault. They don't criticize themselves harshly because they lack criticism, they do this because they don't want to show their anger externally. In fact, they often try their hardest to make sure they don't show anger towards other people.

Type one's strengths:

●**Hard-working**

●**Honest**

●**Independent**

- **Reliable**

- **Accountable**

Type one's weaknesses:

- **Rigidness**

- **Overly-critical**

- **Judgmental**

- **Resentful**

How to Grow Personally

Whether you believe you are at the healthiest level of integration or close to the highest, there is always room for personal growth in your professional and personal life. Below are several pieces of advice which can help you grow as someone with a type one personality.

Keep the Right Mindset

While this will take time and how much time depends on what level you are currently at. Of course, the higher the level, the more time it will take. When I talk about the right mindset, I am talking about several characteristics, such as patience for others, remaining calm, and keeping your emotions in check. Furthermore, most type one personalities think they are always right, which can cause them to become emotional if people don't follow their ways or prove that they are wrong.

Perfectionists are known to be great teachers. However, they often struggle with teaching because they lack patience and consideration for people who do something wrong. But, if you have the right mindset, you will find that you can be an exceptional teacher; you will just have to make sure you have the patience, are able to deal with people who make mistakes, realize that you are not always right, and also realize that perfectionism is not completely possible. While reaching all these factors might seem impossible to you, especially if you have a lower level of integration, you do possess the motivation and drive to make sure you succeed if you become passionate about acquiring the right mindset.

You will want to remain calm. Perfectionists often struggle with keeping their emotions in check. Many perfectionists struggle with keeping their emotions in check because they are highly rigid about how things need to be done. Their primary emotion is anger, which means that they will show more anger than any other emotion. This can cause more problems within the issues already established. Therefore, the calmer you are able to remain, the more you will succeed in keeping your emotions, especially anger, in check. Once you are able to control your anger, you will find it is easier to control other emotions (Cloete, n.d.).

Chapter 6: Using The Enneagram

The Enneagram is more than ordinary personality test. With historical roots dating back to at least the fourteenth century, the modern Enneagram has helped thousands of people discover truths about themselves and their life's purpose. Not only is it an interesting way to learn about yourself, but it's also a catalyst for inspiration and transformation.

The insights that the Enneagram offers can help with many practical life decisions, such as finding a career or lifestyle that suits your personality best. As you learn about your type and watch how it shows up in your life, you may discover that you thrive in a calmer environment than you're currently living in or that your talents would be best used in more people-oriented work than you're doing now. You might recognize habits that get in the way of being your best self, and, as a result, make changes over time.

We'll look at the various parts of the Enneagram symbol and their significance. Then, we'll give an overview of the nine Enneagram types, as well as the core motivations, gifts, and challenges each type possesses. Read on for a deep dive into the human psyche, and a first glimpse at how to harness this powerful knowledge for your own personal growth.

The road to self-discovery

Look at how you react to situations, think about why you act the way you do, analyze your thought processes, and speak to those around you, especially those who know you particularly well. Catch yourself in the moment when you react to a situation, or ask someone to do it for you, and then think back about how you reacted. It might also be helpful to write it all down, in a brainstorming pattern, throwing out random words which sum up the way you felt or reacted at the time.

By nature we are not perfect, but it's also important to remember that we were never designed to be perfect either, every single personality type within The Enneagram has pros and cons – there is no particular type which is better than any of the others.

Don't pick a type which you like the sound of, you'll have been tempted. If you've read through every single type in this book, which you should certainly do, then you will probably have felt yourself connected more so with certain ones; this could be because that is your actual core type calling out to you, or it could be because that is the type of person you strive to become. You have to be honest and identify your true nature.

Remember that you are never 100% one particular type. Every personality type within The Enneagram is influenced by those closely linked to it. For instance, The Peacemaker is quite similar to The Loyalist in many ways, but The Peacemaker might also recognize traits from a different type also. We are all different, and we are never going to fit into a one size fits all box. Your core type is the one you should certainly pay more attention to, however certainly pay attention to your contributing types also, as this means you are much more able to assess yourself as a whole.

Remember to read the helpful tips, as these are designed to enable personal growth. We mentioned that no personality type is perfect, and our tips are there to help address the downsides of your particular type, and help you smooth out the issues which come attached to it. Again, this isn't going to make you a perfect individual, but it will help you deal with some of the more challenging sides of your personality type, and help bring more harmony and happiness to your life.

Assessing other people is a good way to help develop relationships from time to time. Now, this doesn't mean going into analysis mode and questioning everything they do, because this is not going to make them feel particularly comfortable in your presence, however it does mean that you may be able to understand them much better, and help avoid confrontation in the future. Of course, you may also find someone special by doing this too!

Check out some of The Enneagram diagnosis tests we mentioned in our first couple of chapters, as these will help you pinpoint your particular type much easier. Honesty and self-analysis will get you so far, but we are designed as human beings to air on the side of a caution a lot of the time, and these tests will pull out those details we are often not honest about, or those which we like to keep hidden. Whilst they are not 100% accurate, as nothing in life is, they are extremely accurate overall, and can be relied upon to a certain extent, with some personal judgment thrown in for good measure.

It's also useful to remember that although you will begin to develop yourself from using The Enneagram, and from understanding your personality as a result, as we grow and mature, your type could shift a little, and you will move up and down the scale of your particular type as you get older. Nothing is ever static in life, and that means your personality too.

Do not be worried or put off by the sometimes complicated nature of The Enneagram at first. You will more than likely glance upon the diagram and wonder how you're supposed to get your head around it, but after reading this book, you will see that the whole thing becomes much easier, and will start you off on a road to self-discovery.

Yes, lines and wings can complicate matters, but once you have identified your particular type and your particular influences, the road from there begins.

Remember, honesty, perseverance, perhaps a few tears, and some serious determination to be the best version of yourself can be – these are the factors and pushes you need to develop yourself to that higher level, spiritually, professionally, socially, and personally.

Enjoy your road to self-discovery and self-development; hopefully this is a road you will only take once in your life, so pull everything out of it that you can.

Benefits of self-awareness

Your coping skills will improve.

Life will always throw challenges at you. When you lack self-awareness, you may address obstacles from a place of reactivity, and it becomes much harder to cope. With awareness, you can handle these difficulties from a place of grace and acceptance, and it becomes easier to remain positive and relaxed, and to make empowering choices.

You will heal yourself.

When pain remains buried and unaddressed, hurt lingers on in your body, making you more likely to react to the present from the place of your past pain. Working through your challenges makes it easier to act consciously and frees you from the burdens you carry. People tend to feel much better each time an issue gets resolved.

Your internal sense of balance will increase.

Sometimes, you may feel as if you are on an emotional tightrope. Each emotion and reaction has the potential to hit you like a strong gust of wind, leaving you struggling to cling to the delicate balance you've created. Self-awareness gives you strength, and acceptance makes you even stronger. You can maintain your balance and weather internal storms.

Your relationships will get better.

You can make it easy for others to enjoy your company when you relate to them from a place of awareness. When you react to others from a place of unconsciousness, you have more conflicts, and greater hurt may arise in relationships. With self-awareness, you develop compassion for others' pain. It is easier to connect with others from a place of kindness.

You will develop presence and mindfulness.

Being present allows people to live in the here and now. When we are focused on only the current moment, we don't need to feel hurt by the wounds from the past or fear the unknown in the future. We find acceptance and joy in everything. We simply are. In presence, we see others and ourselves fully and compassionately.

Chapter 7: Structure Of The Enneagram

Diagram

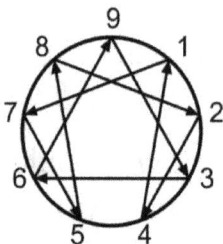

The first step towards understanding the world and people around you is to understand yourself. This is a challenge that many people struggle with. There is a lot that we don't know about ourselves and, with that hindrance, our attempts at understanding other people around us becomes almost impossible. You cannot seek what you don't know, because how will you know that you have found it if you don't know what you were meant to be looking for in the first place?

Understanding the enneagram system will place you on an interesting journey, a journey into self-discovery. The marvels of human nature will enlighten you, astonish you and in some cases probably scare you. You will realize there is much that you never knew about yourself. It will open your eyes to new possibilities and encourage you to recognize your limits, challenges, strengths, and the stimuli in your environment that empower or motivate you.

As you wade through the enneagram, you will learn many things that you can use in your life every day. Like we mentioned earlier, when you learn about yourself, you open your world to new experiences and you learn to understand people better because you look at them from a new enlightened perspective.

Understanding the enneagram structure will introduce positive changes in your life, and give you a new lease of life. The structure of the enneagram might look complex, but it is actually a very simple concept. It features a meshwork of a triangle and an irregular hexagram within a circle. The easiest way to realize the simplicity of this structure is to draw it yourself.

Using a compass, draw a circle. Mark nine points on the circle, each an equal distance away from the other. A circle has 360 degrees, so measure 40 degrees and mark a point, then repeat until you have nine marked along the circumference of the circle.

Label each point with a number, (1 – 9) making sure nine sits at the top. You have now taken the first step towards identifying the nine personality types.

So, before we even consider the triangle or the hexagram, this simple structure already should give you a rough idea of the construct of human personalities. Everything in life comes full circle. Even without digging deep into the theory of the enneagram, you should already be able to surmise the concept of interdependence and the whole.

Once you have completed the enneagram diagram, you will notice that the points are interconnected through smaller lines within the diagram. Take a closer look, and you will notice an equilateral triangle within the circle. This is a triangle with all three sides and angles equal, which is formed by points 3, 6, and 9. The remaining six points interconnect to form an irregular hexagram.

What we can reveal from this diagram is nine different personality types, each connected to each other in some way. What does this tell you about yourself? It is a sign that in the whole you, all the nine personalities might manifest in some way. If you reflect on your life and some of the choices you have made, you should realize that you possess a little bit of every one of them. However, there will be one personality type that stands dominant above the rest. This dominant one is the personality type that defines you. It is the foundation of your being.

Personalities are inborn. They manifest from your childhood and, as you grow older, you embrace your personality type and go on to become the person you are today. Everyone is born with a clean slate. Over the years, many authors and experts on enneagrams have attempted to demystify the concept of personalities. While each expert presents a unique perspective, most believe that everyone is born with a dominant personality type.

This inborn personality becomes your identity. It is through it that you learn how to embrace the environment around you, how to interact with the people you meet, the things you dislike, and activities you are drawn to. The decisions we make are a construct of our subconscious mind. In turn, the subconscious mind is influenced by your dominant personality. This explains why you form some associations with your loved ones and parents, but perhaps have a different perspective of authority and respond differently to affection from other people.

The growth process and personalities are linked. Around the time that children turn six years old, they start to portray unique behavior and responses to different changes in their lives. Their identity starts becoming apparent, and they embrace a new freedom to choose their role in the world.

Generally, the personality type you associate with is a combination of many changes that take place in your life from childhood. Other than genetics, this includes the environment you are brought up in, the defining moments in your life and anything else that may have influenced your growth and development in some way. Because of this, it is safe to say no one is able to just switch their personality from one to another. We all have tiny fragments of all the personality types within us. These manifest differently in the way we respond to different situations in life. This means that it is possible that one of your lesser personalities might suddenly become prominent, perhaps because you find yourself in uncharted territory, as it becomes the only way you can adapt. However, the dominant personality type will always return and persist.

The idea of a dominant personality type can be misleading. By the definition of 'dominant,' you would assume that this particular personality type would dominate your life all the time. However, this is not the case. If you consider all the descriptions and character traits that define your dominant personality type, you will see that it is impossible to manifest all of them all the time. Some of the characteristics may be subtle, whereas others are prominent, so you might not experience the totality of your personality at all times.

Most of the personality traits are expressed in response to someone or something, which we define as a reaction. Your reaction to conflict at home might not be the same as your reaction to conflict at work. The same theory applies to the way you show affection, and how you care for people. Your position or stage in life also influences the way your personality manifests.

Cultural affiliations also have an impact on your personality, because of moral beliefs and the differences in beliefs between cultures. It must be clarified that none of the personalities should be considered superior to the rest. The numerical connotation is simply a neutral designation to eliminate the risk of bias. A number 9 does not mean that this personality is better than a number 3.

There are some traits that each cultural construct holds in high regard. If you demonstrate such traits in your personality, you will be highly favored in these communities. The natural reaction in this scenario will be to embrace the affection and favor, which will, with time, become second nature to you. However, you cannot have too much of anything without some kind of repercussions, right? Take an example of someone who cares deeply about relieving the suffering of others. While you can go out of your way to help people, you can't do it all the time. It will take a toll on you eventually, and while you may be performing an act of kindness, there will be a struggle in other spheres of your life as a result of your good deeds.

The same holds true with personality types. The more you learn about them, the clearer your perception will become. However, awareness of personality types is not complete until you also become aware of their limitations. Personalities and their traits are recommended by different societies in different ways. Does this mean that some personalities are better than others? No, not really. What we can learn from this is that each society has a unique reward scheme that appreciates some traits in some personalities over others.

So where does this leave you, and what can you do about your life? The short answer is self-awareness. Know who you are and what your life is about. Learn about and master the different personality types. Figure out what your personality type is and the characteristic traits that you identify with.

Why is this important? We live in a world where people are struggling to fit in. Thanks to social media, the world is obsessed with appearances, looks and perceptions. Many people live their lives in the shadow of other people, not because they are forced to but because they believe it is the only way to gain fulfillment and satisfaction. This is, however, a fallacy. An imitation by any other name is still just an imitation. Whenever you try to portray yourself as something or someone else, you only succeed at perfecting the lie. With each attempt, you lose grasp of your true self. If you imitate someone for too long, you might end up forgetting your own identity or be ashamed of accepting who you truly are.

Self-awareness is about embracing your true self. You will learn what makes you tick, why you do the things you do and, in the process, learn to appreciate your place in this life. You will understand your value and the value others have in your life.

Discovering Your Personality Type

While we know, there are only nine different personality types; determining the one that best describes you is not that simple. Matters of human personality are not always black and white. As well as the nine main personality types, these are some of the other factors that come into play:

●**Subtypes**

Within each of the nine personality types, there are three variants. Therefore, in theory, there are 27 different characteristics within which you will be able to identify yours. However, given that some of them share very close similarities, this is not one of the easiest things to do.

●Wings

The term 'Wings' in this discussion refers to the adjacent types on either side of each personality type. As you read further into the personality types, you will learn that each personality associates with at least one of the other adjacent personalities. This association has a profound influence on your life, though it is not as great as the dominant personality type. In some cases, both adjacent personality types can influence your life.

●Arrows/lines

Arrows refer to the direction you expect your characteristic behaviors to take in relation to the world around you, whether you are comfortable or you are under stress.

●Development level

The way your personality type manifests also depends on your level of personal growth and development. Individuals who are developed are usually exposed to different levels of maturity, in which case it becomes difficult to identify which category they belong to. Such individuals can portray different characteristics of each personality because they can draw knowledge from their learned and shared experiences, which means they are able to balance their lives and blend in or adapt to different scenarios comfortably.

Given the challenges above, how can you make sure you have a good shot at learning and embracing your personality type? The following discussion will provide you with everything you need to go about this.

Keep an open mind

From the very beginning, you will need to start by eliminating your personal bias towards the enneagram tests or anything else connected with this process. You need to embrace the tests and take them correctly. Don't hold back when answering the questions. After you have the results and you have an idea of what your dominant personality is, make sure you do not rest on your laurels.

You might notice that something within your behavior that does not conform with what you originally believed. This might change your perception of your personality type, especially if you are already in doubt.

Don't obsess over types!

When you read about the different personality types and their unique features, you may fantasize about certain types under the misconception that they are better than the others. The problem here is that you will lose focus on the important facts. These personality tests are not about the different types; they are about you.

Do not approach this from the perspective of characteristics you wish that you have. You are not assigning yourself a type; you are trying to find out what your type is, based on your current predispositions.

Personal bias

It is common for people to come in with preconceptions about themselves when learning about the enneagram of personality types. Often, they will shy away from revealing some of the traits that they consider to be negative. However without admitting such traits, you won't get a true picture of who you are. Remember that the personality tests can only give an accurate or a near-accurate result if you provide it with accurate data.

The risk of ambiguity

As you learn about the personality types, you must be prepared for some ambiguous results. In particular, the peacemaker and the loyalists are two groups that can be easily confused as most of their traits are relatively universal. They could represent almost every other personality type, so you might have a difficult time pointing them out.

As well as this, these two categories don't have very distinct features that you can identify with. If you already are conflicted about a few of the categories, the ambiguity of the peacemaker and loyalist might confuse you even further.

Chapter 8: Ennea-Type Two – "The Helper"

Aliases: The Giver, The Supporter

The Caring, Interpersonal type.

Generally described as:

GenerousPeople-Pleasing DemonstrativePossessive

At their best, Type Twos are described as:

SelflessUnconditionally Loving AltruisticNurturing

Motto: "I must help others. I try to be loved by loving."

The Helper in General

People who exhibit a Core Type Two have a strong desire to love and be loved, and actively work to please people around them. They place a high priority on the "good" and "true" things in life, such as love, friendship, family, and community. Type Two people genuinely desire to help others and are concerned about being perceived as helpful.

They are often sentimental and loyal, even to the point of self-sacrifice. Helpers rarely break away from relationships without traumatically severing the bond with the person.

When a Type Two person can fully engage and express themselves, they become the caring, nurturing center for their groups of family, friends, and social circles. They enjoy caring for others during times of stress and illness, selflessly sacrificing their time and interests to ensure the people in their lives are happy, safe, and provided for. They make excellent emotional "harbors" for others in difficult times, as it is naturally easy for them to be accepting, warm, consoling, and nonjudgmental.

Sometimes, while a Type Two person is working to develop a relationship with someone, they can become possessive and jealous if the person doesn't display the same emotional intensity or commitment.

They greatly fear rejection and will change themselves or ignore their needs to gain affection from others. Helpers prefer to be seen as needed – a pillar of support and a generous source of acceptance for the people they love.

When a Type Two person can develop a relationship of give-and-take with others, in which both people are mutually loving, they feel fulfilled. Their natural generosity is self-rewarding, and they receive pleasure from expressing and acting on the concern and love they have for others. Doing "good" for others makes a Helper feel worthwhile.

How Helpers See Themselves vs. How Others See Them

Helpers see themselves as genuinely invested in the best interests of others, but they can also become attached, jealous, and resentful of the time and energy they invest. They think they are driven by a true desire to be helpful – highly altruistic – but actually Helpers generally operate under pressure to do the "right thing." They often seek reassurance that they are "worthy" of love. While the Helper believes that their self-sacrifice is pure, other people may see the sacrifice as manipulative, or as a way to try to "buy" love.

Helpers are highly invested in seeing themselves as helpful, sometimes despite the feedback they receive. While they think others may not recognize it, this drive to help others and be acknowledged for it can cause Type Two people a great deal of anxiety.

Because Type Two people are so in-tune to the levels of acceptance from others, they may use self-deceptive techniques to protect their pride. They prefer to think of themselves in glowing, positive terms and can be highly sensitive to rejection. Then, some Type Two people repress or compartmentalize their personality. With too much of this, the Helper's anger can build up over time, eventually erupting in a dramatic event.

While the Helper Ennea-type can see themselves as the embodiment of loving actions – because, in their view, they always put others first – they can come across as needy or manipulative at times. The Helper can see themselves as the facilitator or manager of the relationships in their lives, however it may appear to others that the Type Two person is overly involved in other people's business. While the Type Two person may find fulfillment in caring for others, it can be frustrating to others when the Type Two person begins to pull back and direct their energies toward something else.

The "Average" Helper's Mental Health

When a Helper is at an average level of health, they feel a need to be needed. They are open and giving, but also expect a return of their outward energy, which can send confusing messages to others. Sometimes intrusive and possessive,

Helpers at this level tend to exhibit some co-dependent tendencies, while also priding themselves on what they do and how helpful they are to others.

When a Helper is feeling better than average, they may be full of the best intentions for those around them, while coming across as intrusive or demanding. At this level of health, a Helper wants everyone to feel good about themselves and is quick to hand out flattery and approval of others, but they may be sensitive when people don't return their open emotional expressions.

Moving Toward Integration: Helpers At Their Best

When moving in their Direction of Integration (growth) and exhibiting their best qualities, Helpers become selfless, displaying high levels of emotional intelligence, and can shed their pride and narcissism.

Basic Desire(s): To feel loved and appreciated

Basic Motivation(s): To be loved, needed, and appreciated; to express feelings for others and elicit a response, to justify their claims about themselves.

Unique Gift(s): Generous, sensitive to others' needs and emotions, and creative with their energy, which can make them incredibly romantic. They work hard to show their support and loyalty to those they love.

Basic Goal: To connect with love through deep relationships.

Generous, considerate, and charming, a Type Two person at their best makes people feel at home. They make others feel good about themselves; they make others feel secure. They are reliable, compassionate, and above all, helpful. They assist, they support, and they love with respect.

When a Helper's Mental Health is Excellent

When at their best, Helpers are altruistic, giving unconditional love to themselves and others. They become unselfish and humble, recognizing the privilege they enjoy being a part of the lives of others. Compassionate, caring, and thoughtful, they embody encouragement and appreciation, and their connectivity is less needy, less absorbing of other people's energy, and becomes a source of inspiration and support for others.

As Type Two people disintegrate, they shift their connective energy with others to a more demanding interaction, which can make them "needy" or "high-maintenance." Although they enjoy and find fulfillment in helping others meet their needs, they can become demanding and resentful that they give energy to others without receiving the same levels of energy in return.

Moving Toward Disintegration: Helpers When Stressed

When moving in their Direction of Disintegration (stress), the normally nurturing and empathetic Helper regresses toward becoming dominating and self-absorbed.

Basic Fear(s): Afraid of being unwanted and/or unworthy of being loved

Triggering Emotion: **Pride**

Becomes Fixated On: **Flattery**

Needy, manipulative, and demanding, a Type Two person under stress is imaging themselves constantly in their most terrifying truth: they are worthless. When a Helper feels unloved or unappreciated, they doubt their own value and to work to "win" or "earn" love from others. They expect sacrifices to be rewarded with love and appreciation, although they try to hide it. They are false and selfish, but most of all, they need help. When a Helper feels neither love nor respect, they are desperate for assistance and support.

What Type Two People Might Struggle With

Type Two people can suffer from emotional repression, resentment, or bitterness related to not receiving the love they feel they deserve.

At times, Type Twos can become manipulative in order to get the attention they seek and can develop different personas for different groups of people in order to "earn" love and acceptance from each. A Type Two person might spend time and energy ignoring or "pushing aside" their authentic self, to the point they feel controlled by their relationships and long for freedom from them.

Type Twos tend to overlook or ignore their own needs when seeking emotion from others. Possessiveness, jealousy, and manipulative behaviors can complicate their intense need to be loved.

When Helper's Mental Health is Struggling

When fully disintegrated and under stress, Helpers become bitter and entitled, feeling their suffering is not appreciated; they are not receiving the love they "deserve." They can suffer from emotional binge eating or addictive behaviors, to seek out the joy they aren't getting from their personal connections.

As Helpers decrease their stress and focus on their health, they become less angry and manipulative, more honest about their own motives and the motivations of others. The healthier the Helper's mindset, the less they will focus on the love they aren't receiving and begin to focus on the love they have to give.

Potential Addictive Struggles

Type Two people might struggle with addictions to food and can binge eat under stress. In some cases, feelings of being unloved or unworthy can lead to eating disorders.

Some Type Two people struggle with addictions to medications or alcohol, attempting to find pleasure in a substance instead of a person. In order to get attention and sympathy, an unhealthy Type Two person may engage in faking illnesses or exhibit hypochondria.

Overcoming Challenges of the Helper Ennea-Type

It's important that the Helper take time to take care of themselves. Self-care is essential for a Helper, because if a Type Two is not taking care of themselves, they simply can't care for others. Rest, proper diet, and loving actions toward themselves can help the Helper stay balanced and at their best.

Being The Best Helper

Harness the best aspects of your Helper Ennea-type and diminish negative traits that emerge under stress. If you're a Helper, or know someone who is, consider how the following techniques can help you unlock and grow the best version of yourself.

Practice Listening

Type Two people need to give themselves proper credit. They love deeply, and sometimes they can't recognize or accept care from others. To maintain balance, a Helper must hear and absorb other people's affections and support, and they must learn to take "no" for an answer when their help isn't needed. Helpers struggle to let go of the need for attention, so learning to listen to others may involve learning to understand other people's emotions when they don't "look" the way the Helper expects.

Type Two people find joy in listening to others' true perspectives, especially if they can use those perspectives to counteract their internal self-doubt. Individual or group therapy can teach a Type Two to actively engage with others' communication styles. In particular, studying people's "Love Languages" can really sharpen a Helper's empathy and ability to connect.

Suggestions:

Focus on doing something quiet – to hear other languages. Listen to international music or nature sounds (rain, ocean shores, bird songs, etc.). Listen to a podcast or nonfiction audio book, especially something motivational or comical. Practice yoga or meditation. Study and apply knowledge of the Love Languages.

There are simple things a Helper can do to hone their ability to hear and connect with positivity in themselves, especially when they give themselves freedom from the pressure to "fix the situation" for the person they're listening to.

Practice Clear Communication

Type Two people naturally love to communicate, and when they refine these skills, they make huge impacts on the people around them. The Helper at their best finds joy in clearly demonstrating and expressing their love. They are fulfilled when other people acknowledge their caring words and actions.

Although a Helper can become frustrated when trying to express themselves, learning to choose their words to connect with others in a way they understand will help the Helper increase their feelings of social love and acceptance.

Suggestions:

Study a new language – learn words and phrases people respond to. Become aware of your motivations and practice directing your energy. Express your expectations and disappointments, without becoming emotional. When a job is done, congratulate yourself, then release other people from any "obligation" to acknowledge you.

There are simple things a Helper can do to release their thoughtful, intuitive, nurturing energy, especially when they give themselves permission to be themselves.

Chapter 9: Subtypes In The Enneagram

About The 27 Subtypes

As with most personality typing systems, the Enneagram can sometimes feel incomplete if you try to view yourself as just one whole Enneatype. The development of subtypes within each Enneatype help you to understand your personality type and where you are at in your evolution at a far deeper level. We are not just a single Enneatype. AT any given time, we can travel up and down our evolutionary ladder around the circle based on times of stress or security.

Subtypes of each Enneatype are broken into three basics for understanding. We have those aspects of our selves that show us how we deal with self-preservation, social situations, and one-to-one relationships, which can also include our sexual nature. These subtypes can be considered our most basic instincts for survival in each category. It is how we instinctively react in these situations, without thought.

We each have these subtypes within our personality Enneatype; however, these usually develop naturally, in a different priority level for each of us. The subtype we can most readily identify within our Enneatype is often what is considered our dominant subtype; the second would be our secondary, while the third is often found to be our repressed subtype.

These subtypes can also be viewed with an eye of where we go when we stress or succeed our Disintegration and Integration points. By knowing where we go to at an instinctual level, we can begin to develop and evolve ourselves into healthier, more balanced individuals, and strengthen our relationships with the rest of the world.

Ones: The Perfectionist

Self-Preservation Ones: The Pioneer

Self-Preservation Ones can be very warm and friendly, but they are also the most worried and anxious types of the Enneagram. Their focus is on perfectionism and will work hard to make everything perfect. This focus on work is often used to cover the anxiety they have for always feeling they, themselves, are less than perfect. They want to impose order on all that is around them for what they feel is always doing the right thing.

Social Ones: The Social Reformer

When on their own home court, the Social Reformer Ones are very outgoing and friendly. They have a hard time adapting to things not done in ways that they feel are the "right way," and can be both critical and resentful of others not following their perceived set of proprietary rules. These Ones can be good teachers, and they see themselves in that role, always trying to teach others their image of perfect. They are often socially correct, but their hindrance lies in their inability to change and adapt.

One-To-One Ones: The Evangelist

The One-to-One Ones have a zealousness unmatched by other Enneatypes or subtypes. Where Ones tend to focus on making themselves perfect, these Ones have a focus more on bringing others, and the rest of society, to a state of perfection. They pay a great deal of attention to whether they perceive others as doing, or not doing things right, according to their own very strict standards. They also have a deep jealous nature, not only for those they love or are partners with but also for those who may have a greater amount of self-expression.

Twos: The Giver

Self-Preservation Twos: The Nurturer

Self-Preservation Twos are very nurturing and connect with many different people on many levels, although they tend to be a little more afraid about making those connections than other Twos. The side of their nurturing, however, can come at a cost to those they care for. Their nurturing takes on a form of entitlement for care in getting their own needs met. In actuality, their charm is turned on in a nurturing style without conscious awareness that their true motives are to be taken care of as a result.

Social Twos: The Ambassador

Social Twos play to the recognition of their accomplishments and like to prove their value by stepping in and taking charge. They take on what they can to make themselves invaluable to others, using their ambition to gain recognition and self-esteem. Although being on center stage for these individuals is not always as important to them as making the right connections to further their ambitions.

One-To-One Twos: The Lover

One-to-One Twos can have two distinct sides, one of either aggression or the use of seduction to gain attention and recognition in personal relationships and interactions. They strive to be generous and make themselves attractive to win the approval of their selected target, even if they plan to make it a short-term goal or relationship. Their tone is often seductive, although not necessarily of a sexual nature. The One-to-One Two can be more passionate and emotional than others Twos and has no problem bringing attention to their appeal ability and promises of support to win the attraction and approval of others.

Threes: The Performer

Self-Preservation Threes: The Company Man/Woman

Self-Preservation Threes tend to immerse themselves into work and whatever else it may take to achieve material success and security for themselves and anyone around them. They are all about image, although they do not like tooting their own horn, because they do not feel that is a good image to project. They like to look good and show themselves as "good" to the social spectrum they are connected to. They are results-oriented people who work hard and prove themselves very self-sufficient.

Social Threes: The Politician

Social Threes know instinctively how to climb the social ladder, and do so in order to achieve the material and other status symbols that society views as markers of having the right "image." These Threes can be true social leaders, or they may just have the ability for hype and propaganda, forcing others to see the image they want to be projected. Prestige and social success are the epitomes of being in the winners' circle for this highly competitive subtype.

One-To-One Threes: The Movie Star

One-to-One Threes are less focused on their own personal successes, as they are on supporting the successes of their partners and others around them. The success of their image comes with a focus on either femininity or masculinity, and how well they are perceived as such. They have strong ties to gender issues and identity, although they may have some confusion when it comes to their own contemplation of these same issues. They are very strong team players with powerful charisma.

Fours: The Romantic

Self-Preservation Fours: The Creative Individualist

Self-Preservation Fours search for authenticity in everything around them and will go at great lengths to find it, even to the point of being reckless. These unorthodox creative types have no problem throwing caution to the wind and just picking up and jumping into a new place or situation if they feel the need for self-preservation. They may appear stoic on the outside, but inside they can be highly emotionally sensitive. Their feelings and emotions can run dark, and they are afraid to share that side of themselves with others. Their tolerance for frustration is high, and even though they may stress to feelings of anxiety or sadness, they try to tough things out and put on a happy face to the world.

Social Fours: The Critical Commentator

Social Fours focus on the intensity and authenticity of their own emotions versus societal expectations. They are highly critical of themselves, and when they compare themselves to others, they usually feel that they are lacking or not worthy in some way or another. This deficiency is often felt when in social situations, and they tend toward feelings of enviousness at the easier way that others seem to fit in, or seem to belong. They have strong inclinations in the validity of their emotions, and may sometimes wear their heart on their sleeve.

One-To-One Fours: The Dramatic Person

One-to-One Fours are highly competitive and take the strengths of others as a personal challenge to come out on top in any situation. If they do not feel stronger than the other person, more accomplished does, falling short on a tally of achievements, their personal value suffers. One-to-One Fours can sometimes come off as aggressive, and will always list their achievements as being better than another's. They will use power or style to beat the competition and to create within themselves the ability to move forward with their own personal agenda.

Fives: The Observer

Self-Preservation Fives: The Castle Defender

Self-Preservation Fives can be of one of two types. They can either use their home as their personal castle or fortress—a place where they retreat to with feelings of safety. Alternatively, they may forego having an attachment to any single place and spend their time moving around or traveling. Even so, there is a need for either type to have a private space for alone time when they feel the need. Self-Preservation Fives can be very friendly and have a genuine warmth. They like to keep their needs minimal and have all that they may need or want at any time within the safety of their private haven.

Social Fives: The Professor

Social Fives thrive on acquiring knowledge and work hard to become experts in the fields or areas that they find of interest. They very much enjoy connecting with those who may share the same causes they believe in, or have common ground in their intellectual interests. This may lead to them having stronger connections with these people, then they may have with those they have around them as family, friends, or otherwise. Their ability to participate with others in a given situation can be hindered by their tendency to over-think, over-analyze, and observe, offering their knowledge as a form of teaching that often comes from study as opposed to experience.

One-To-One Fives: The Secret Agent

One-to-One Fives can be inwardly more emotionally connected or aware than any other aspect of the Five Enneatype. This still doesn't usually mean they show it outwardly but tend to only share that secretive side of themselves in an intimate setting. While they struggle with a preference to maintain autonomy, they also want to share that secret, emotional side of themselves with another being with whom they feel an intimate emotional connection. These Five types can have a flair for the romantic that may demonstrate itself in some form of artistic or creative expression.

Sixes: The Loyal Skeptic

Self-Preservation Sixes: The Family Loyalist

Self-Preservation Sixes tend toward more of the flight side of the fight or flight spectrum. They constantly question and doubt things and circumstances to try to find a sense of comfort and certainty to feel safer and secure in any given situation. They look to others outside themselves for protection and work in a friendly manner with affection and warmth to attract those they would see as protective allies.

Social Sixes: The Social Guardian

Social Sixes have a need for clarity about their role in society or even in a group. They need clear boundaries and rules set for social interaction, because they fear rejection, and have the need to know how to avoid it. They have a strong sense of duty and will live up to it, although depending on the situation, it can feel like either a calling or a burden. Social Sixes are far more logical and rational than Self-Preservation Sixes, which helps them to be certain and confident. They like to focus on making benchmarks, and finding reference points to ensure they live up to the protection from the outside sources that they feel they need.

One-To-One Sixes: The Warrior

Where Self-Preservation Sixes lean toward the flight side of the fight or flight spectrum, One-to-One Sixes jump to the fight side of the equation. The saying that the best defense is a good offense is very applicable to One-to-One Sixes, and they quickly leap to defend their ideologies and idealism fiercely. This can easily turn them into the role of risk-takers or rebels, and they use their contrary nature to create control and stability in their lives to deal with their underlying fears, even though they may not be aware that these fears exist.

Sevens: The Epicure

Self-Preservation Sevens: The Gourmand

Self-Preservation Sevens enjoy good conversation, spending quality family time, planning and implementing fun projects and dining out or sharing elaborately prepared food with others. They are more hedonistic than most other Enneatypes or subtypes and can lean toward over-stimulation in their quest for enjoyment. Their lifestyle leans toward one of abundance, and they enjoy sharing it with others. They have an instinctive knowledge of how to make things happen, which makes them regularly successful at getting and achieving what they want from life.

Social Sevens: The Utopian Visionary

The Seven Enneatype is a planner who does not like putting limitations on the expansion of their own personal awareness and achievements, so the Social Seven is quite the dichotomy, with their need for expression of the love of life and their social ideals through others, such as groups and friends. They do not want to appear that the only interests they have are their own or that they are opportunistic. Social Sevens dedicate themselves in service to others around them as a way of pushing aside their own personal desires in the present. They prefer to show themselves to the world as those who would ease the suffering of others.

One-To-One Sevens: The Adventurer

One-to-One Sevens are optimistically enthusiastic dreamers with a passionate need to see things as they would want or imagine them to be as opposed to the reality that is truly before them. They jump right on board with a fascinated attraction to a new adventure, but this fascination also carries weight with new people or new ideas that come across their path. One-to-One Sevens are highly suggestible and easily excited. However, they can just as easily raise the suggestibility levels in others with their personal charm.

Eights: The Protector

Self-Preservation Eights: The Survivalist

Self-Preservation Eights are far more suited to a hostile world than a friendly one. Their focus is on whatever it is that they feel needed to survive. They fight to win, especially when it comes to protecting themselves, personal space, or family, and will go down fighting to achieve that win, if necessary. They are not the types to give in! Self-Preservation Eights get frustrated easily, especially when they feel what they want or want to achieve is not happening in a timely enough fashion.

Social Eights: The Group Leader/Gang Leader

The often-rebellious Social Eights are leaders who are fierce and loyally committed to their preference for social causes and friends. The usual aggression, often fueled by anger, found in the Eight Enneatype is softened by their need to care for others, and will harness their aggression to lead their group toward a common goal or agenda. To those that they feel are in need of support, they are protective mentor types and will move the feelings and needs of others to a higher place on their priority list than their own.

One-To-One Eights: The Commander

Also in possession of an often-rebellious nature, One-to-One Eights find preference in being right at the center of whatever is going on. This subtype has a strong tendency toward possession for the sake of control and can prove quite forceful about it, even (or especially) when this applies to a personal partner. They enjoy the power they can hold over the various situations and people they encounter. Their true drive is for surrender, and seek that special someone to whom they would find themselves comfortable enough with to just let go and surrender.

Nines: The Mediator

Self-Preservation Nines: The Collector

Self-Preservation Nines have an appetite for material consumption, and whether this is food or just "things," they can find themselves doing and/or collecting anything that will take their focus away from their own personal needs. Familiar routines and daily rhythms guide the comfort levels of Self-Preservation Nines, and they like to ground themselves by losing themselves in whatever activity will keep them otherwise preoccupied.

Social Nines: The Community Benefactor

Social Nines seek comfort and belonging in social circles and groups. Their light-hearted and fun style tends to blend well with others, and Social Nines will do whatever they can, and whatever it takes to prove themselves invaluable for their admittance to being part of the group. This subtype can show themselves to be great leaders, willing to work for the common agenda of the group toward good. They still have the tendency, like most Nine types, to forget any focus on personal priorities and/or needs.

One-To-One Nines: The Seeker

One-to-One Nines have a focus on merging with something or someone outside of themselves, including nature as a possibility of reaching a more transcendent state. These Nines are relationship-oriented and sweet natured. They do lack an assertiveness when it comes to self and have a hard time maintaining personal boundaries and a sense of individual self. They can easily find themselves taking on or adapting to the opinions and feelings of those who are important and close to them.

Chapter 10: How The Enneagram Ties In With Your Personality

We have already mentioned that the nine points of the Enneagram represent one of the nine possible personality types according to this system however, humans are complicated beings, and there are many things that intertwine in making us unique. In other words, no single person is only marked by a single personality type. We are all likely to have a combination of different personality types within us, with one or two of them being viewed as distinctly more prominent than the rest. The one personality type that stands out more than any other will be known as your 'basic personality type', the one that you will base most of your decisions and understanding of yourself on. However, as you become more and more familiar with the Enneagram, it will be a good idea to have a close look at the other personality types that represent you as well at some point in the future.

From birth, we being our lives with a certain personality type this is sometimes referred to as our temperament, which determines some of the basic reactions that we will have to the world that surrounds us. As we grow a little older and we begin to interact with other people, we develop a very specific personality type from a very early age. It only takes a few years on Earth for the people around us to recognize the kind of personality that we are likely to have for the remainder of our lives. This is why you will so often hear people describing you know the same way as when you were a child.

This primary personality type is the essence of the Enneagram, and it will determine how we interact with other children and how we develop our own place in the school yard. Not to mention later on at work. The interesting thing about personalities is that we may not even be aware of the fact that we have a particular one. In fact, if you do not develop an interest in the study of psychology throughout your life, you may be completely oblivious to the personality type that defines who you are. As a result, there are likely to be many things about your life and the people around you that you will not be able to understand or to answer unless you spend a little more time learning how to get to know yourself better.

Another curious thing that your primary personality type has an effect on is based on the things that you have an instinctive reaction to, as well as your likes and dislikes. For example, it determines your relationship with food, how organized you are, your daily hygiene rituals, and how much space you need to feel comfortable when there are other people around you. Curiously, even though more and more research is always being developed into the realization and growth of different personality types, we actually still don't know why they develop in the first place or why there are only nine of them to cover almost every single human being on earth. In fact, since there are so many people on the planet, the logical conclusion might be that there are likely to be hundreds of different personality types available around the world. However, this is not the case, which is bizarre considering how many different nations and cultures there are around the globe.

Thus, by the time you reach the age of five years old, there will be many things about your consciousness that will already be predetermined for the rest of your life. Unless you were to go through a major psychological change or an accident, you will likely not change your personality type at all for the rest of your life.

Important Things to Know About Your Basic Personality Type

Since we mentioned that it is important to take this research into your personality type one step at a time, we must also mention that there are a number of important things that you need to keep in mind when you do finally discover what your primary personality type actually is. The reason why we mention this here and now instead of mentioning it later on is because, this way, you will be less likely to specifically focus on that one single personality type that appears and nothing else. Remember, you are a complex creature, and it takes a number of different things combined together in order to show you a more objective image of who you really are.

The following are very important points that you must keep in mind after you discover your primary personality type. Keep these at the back of your mind at all times, especially when you are done going through the Enneagram for the very first time.

You will not be jumping from one personality type to another as you move through the system. This is why we mentioned that it is so important that you understand that your personality has been predetermined a long time ago even if you were not aware of it at the time. This is also why we mentioned that you should always complete the Enneagram with a clear mind and a state where you feel the most like yourself, so that there would not be any part of the outside world that would interfere with your honest results.

There is no such thing as a personality type that is inherently male or female. Therefore, even if you happen to live in a culture where certain behaviors may be attributed to either one gender or the other, this is not the case with the Enneagram. Instead, you should read each personality type as one that can be equally applied to both men and women. They are also equally applied to people of all ages and from anywhere in the world, so do not allow the descriptions to feel in any way limiting to the things that you could do or achieve in life. The best way to overcome this potential problem is to treat the personality descriptions as if they were only referring to you and no one else in the world, because this will allow you to truly view them within yourself and not be influenced by any other people.

You may notice that there will be certain small aspects of the personality description which may or may not apply to you at the specific time of when you are reading these descriptions. This is something that can happen if you are not in the usual state that you are normally in from the perspective of your own psychology. This refers to the states of extreme happiness or extreme sadness, where you are much less likely to be able to view yourself from an objective point of view. Again, the best way to deal with this is to not look for answers from the Enneagram at times when you are not feeling like your true self. Even though this may sound like a slightly bizarre thing to look for, it is interesting to note that we all have that inherent feeling of feeling like ourselves and not feeling like ourselves, which is why it is important to be able to follow that instinct.

You should keep in mind that the number 1 to 9 which are used in the Enneagram do not in any way denote anything positive or negative about any particular personality type. They are simply there as a number to denote a difference between one type or another, but certainly not to denote whether one personality type is better or worse. Keep in mind that these numbers do not in any way represent any kind of scale, which is why you should never treat them as such. There should be no reason for you to be encouraged or discouraged for getting a particular number as a personality type.

Likewise, there is also no such thing as a god personality or a bad personality type. Do not allow your results to sway you into thinking that you are a bad person, or for that matter, that you are a better person than someone else. If a personality type seems at all more desirable than another it is simply because the environment that you are finding yourself in has somehow made one type culturally more appropriate than another. However, this way of understanding personalities is truly completely false. Each type is part of who we are as human beings. In fact, we are able to be diverse and even more unique specifically because there are different personality types to choose from. The world would be a very boring place if we were all the same and if we all had the same interests and dislikes. In fact, so many things that make up who we are as people, as well as all the technological advancements that have happened over time, are due in large part to the fact that there is such variety in who we are as individuals.

A Final Note Before We Begin

No matter what anyone else may say about you or your personality, remember that the whole point of this process is for you to discover who you are and to be unique. You are not meant to change anything about yourself regardless of which personality you turn out to be. You are also certainly not expected to try and be anyone else at all. You are who you have always been and that is something that will never change. The Enneagram is only here to help you learn even more about yourself, so that you can better understand your own individuality and why it is so important for the world that you are who you are.

Chapter 11: Type Two: The Giver

Overview

Givers face a certain paradox in terms of what it actually means to be a true Giver. These people can be genuinely helpful to the people around them, but when they are not completely healthy, they are obsessed with giving insofar as they want to be perceived as helpful (whether or not they actually help or even harm others). Givers thrive on trying to go out of their way to help others and on being abundantly generous. For them, this is the most significant, most valuable way to experience everyday life. Healthy Givers feel genuine concern for people and want to do good. Feeling love within themselves allows them to spread more love to others. It is also what makes them feel as if they are worthwhile. The type two is primarily concerned with love, intimacy, sharing with others, and nurturing family, and close friendships.

A balanced and healthy Giver is able to be kind, helpful, generous, and aware of other people's needs and wants. Other people are attracted to them in a way that feels almost magnetic. Balanced givers are able to help others feel warmth just from their proximity. They have the gift of knowing how to energize others through their gifts (both material and spiritual). They know how to shower healthy attention and appreciation on their loved ones, and how to help them to recognize the most positive qualities in themselves that perhaps had been ignored. Basically, healthy Givers are the archetype of the ideal parent that every child dreams of. They are able to see others in their truest state, to comprehend them without a shred of judgment, and never seems to be short on patience. As their name suggests, the Giver is always happy to extend a helping hand. They also share the remarkable ability to know exactly how and when to let go – like a parent helping a young child learn to ride a bicycle without training wheels. The true gift of the Healthy Twos is that they know how to open the hearts of even the most repressed individual. Their ears are already so open that their example teaches us the way to be more thoroughly and complexly human.

The difficulty that the Giver faces comes in terms of their inner development. The dark side of the Giver that can limit their inner development involves pride, deception of themselves and of others, and a lack of boundaries. The Giver might experience the irresistible need to become too involved in other people's lives. This might transform into the negative habit of actually working to manipulate other people in order to get their own emotional needs met. It is necessary to explore these dark places in order to effect actual transformation. However, the Giver does not like to acknowledge such dark places in themselves as it contradicts their sense of self as wholly positive, even idealized to the point of sainthood.

This need to face a fear of worthlessness is undoubtedly the biggest obstacle facing Givers (as well as Types Three and Types Four). All three types project an outward image of confidence. However, beneath the surface, they all fear that they have no intrinsic value in themselves and, therefore, they have to be or to do something above and beyond, if they are to win love and acceptance from others. When Givers are veering towards the unhealthy realm of their personalities, they work to cultivate a deceptive image of being wholly unselfish, self-sacrificing and generous. They act as though they do not want any kind of gratification for themselves. This is contrary to the truth, which is that they often have very high and unrealistic expectations, coupled with unacknowledged emotional needs.

When a Giver veers towards the unhealthy end of the spectrum, they are insatiable in their need to seek validation. Under the tutelage of their superego's demands, they sacrifice everything they can in order to make other people love them. When they put other people before themselves and act loving and unselfish, they think that automatically makes them entitled to unconditional love. Unfortunately, when they constantly put others first, they naturally become secretly angry and resentful. These feelings contradict their identity as Giver, so they work diligently to repress them. Inevitably, the Giver will erupt, whether through an emotional outburst that can even appear to be a childish tantrum or through more subtle passive-aggressive behaviors. These outbursts tend to do great damage to the Givers' relationships, as it threatens to uncover the true motives for their generous, loving behavior, which makes them appear inauthentic to their loved ones.

The connected types of the Giver are:

Wing: Perfectionist 1

Wing: Performer 3

Security Type: Romantic 4

Stress Type: Protector 8

The non-connected, look-alike types of the Giver are:

Epicure 7

Mediator 9

The probability of types (other types to consider if Giver is your top choice):

65% Giver

8% Epicure

8% Mediator

7% Romantic

5% Perfectionist

The 65% percent chance assigned to the Giver type means that there is a high chance you are a Giver if you received a high score. However, you should still review whether your second and third choices match the other probable types (Epicure, Mediator, Romantic and Perfectionist). Remember, if a certain type has a strong wing of one or the other, that can greatly influence how the personality manifests itself. If you cannot accept the type you are, your feelings may be legitimate, or could be a result of the negative stereotypes you have heard about the type, so make sure to explore any strong reactions you may have.

Myths About the Giver

The Giver has a bad reputation of giving because he or she has an ulterior motive: To get something in return. Givers are also associated with being dependent, and even needy.

Adjectives that Describe the Giver

The positive adjectives include: Responsible, insightful, flexible, optimistic, generous, loving, kind, sensitive to people's feelings, and nurturing. The negative adjectives include: Indirect, overly proud, intrusive, hysterical, and dramatic.

The Underlying Truths of the Giver

The basic principle the giver has forgotten: That the needs of all people are naturally met in the universe's flow of giving and receiving.

The giver wrongly believes: The only way to get is to give and the only way to be loved is through being needed.

The giver created these behaviors to compensate: In order to get their needs met, the Giver tried to make themselves indispensable, overlooking their own needs and wants.

The Characteristics that Define the Giver

Because of these adaptive behaviors, the Giver focuses on: First and foremost, other people and relationships, at the expense of their own personal identity.

They put their energy into: Figuring out what people need and want and trying to anticipate their needs. Finding and maintaining romantic relationships. Keeping the respect and positive praise of other people.

They desperately try to avoid: Rejection, disappointment, a lack of appreciation and the possibility of being discarded.

They have these strengths: They are generous, giving and helpful. They are sensitive to other people's needs and wants. They are always expressive in their appreciation of others. They are supportive and highly energetic.

They communicate in the following way: The Giver is expressive and generous in giving advice to loved ones. This style might appear intrusive, but it can also be friendly and helpful.

The Sources of Stress, Anger and Defensiveness

They are stressed by: Being pulled in all sorts of directions based on their insatiable need to give, not knowing their actual needs, and having their needs unmet.

They are angered about: Constantly feeling like their needs are not being met.

They are defensive towards: Feeling unappreciated or controlled by others

Their anger and defensiveness are characterized as such: Via unpredictable outbursts that appear uncharacteristic. Outburst might include tears and accusations thrown against loved ones.

Personal Growth

Their final goal is: To begin to understand that the important thing in terms of being loved is being themselves, and that giving and receiving is part of the natural flow of the universe.

They can further this growth by:

Understanding what unconditional love is.

Identifying the need to flatter others and obtain approval.

Recognizing their own needs rather than focusing on the needs of others.

Trying not to be everyone's "best friend."

Being attentive when trying to be helpful might appear to be controlling.

Identifying their personal limits so they do not burn out.

Their biggest obstacle is: Guilt. This might manifest itself in terms of negative feelings that arise when the Giver tries to meet his or her own needs. The Giver is further blocked by always seeking to rationalize what needs to be done for others before doing things for themselves. Even when the Giver is offered something, he or she is likely to refuse it, even if it is what they truly want.

Others can support this growth by:

Appreciating the Giver themselves, rather than becoming dependent on what he or she has to give.

Checking in regularly on what they need and want.

Regularly saying thank you and specifically telling them exactly what you appreciate about them.

Taking an interest in their problems, even if they try to avoid talking about them

being gentle with criticism.

Reassuring them about your feelings.

Encouraging them to say no, set limits and enforce boundaries.

Famous Givers

(including many actors, musicians and philanthropists):

Priscilla Presley, Leo Buscaglia, Dolly Parton, Danny Thomas, Luciano Pavarotti, Monica Lewinsky, Nancy Reagan, Richard Thomas "John Boy Walton," Jennifer Tilly, Kenny G, Martin Sheen, Josh Groban, Eleanor Roosevelt, Barry Manilow, Juliette Binoche, Bobby McFerrin, Richard Simmons, John Denver, Ann Landers,

Paula Abdul, Arsenio Hall, Pope John XXIII, Byron Katie, Bishop Desmond Tutu, Lionel Richie, Stevie Wonder, Music of Journey, Elizabeth Taylor, and Danny Glover.

Related Types

Every personality type is influenced by the wings to the point that they might blend into one of them. If a personality type has a strong wing, it will make a huge impact on the individual's personality.

Perfectionist 1 (wing): When a Giver has a stronger Perfectionist wing, they can be more idealistic, objective and judgmental. The two types have similarly high standards and can focus intensively on the health of others. They are both masterful at suppressing their desires. However, whereas Perfectionists try to improve others based on their internal, inflexible standards, the Giver will change him or herself to make the other person happy.

Performer 3 (wing): These two types are doubly related because they belong to the same Heart Center type, which causes them to share certain personality traits. Givers and Performers both tend to be "doers" who are full of energy and eager to get things done. They share a high degree of energy and a willingness to adapt to whatever circumstance. These two types are different because Givers are always thinking about other people's needs and wants, while Performers are so intent on getting things done that, they will push aside other people's feelings. When a Giver has a stronger Performer wing, they can be more self-assured, ambitious and competitive.

Romantic 4 (security type): These two types are doubly related because they belong to the same Heart Center type, which causes them to share certain personality traits. (Note, the Giver is the stress type of the Romantic). These two types are very keyed in to other people's feelings. They can be overly sensitive and are very committed to their relationships.

Their high degree of emotional intensity can make them ideal romantic partners and talented artists. Their main difference is that Givers are more focused on external factors, while Romantics tend to look inside and can tend towards depression. When a Giver moves toward the positive side of four, they are able to acknowledge their negative feelings and find new sources of self-value aside from helping others. When they move to the negative side of four, they can be even more judgmental of themselves compared to others and tend towards self-absorption and depression.

Protector 8 (stress type): These types are closely related because the Giver is the security type of the Protector and the Protector is the stress type of the Giver. These two types are also similar because they both have energetic personalities that tend towards generosity and protectiveness. Both types are attracted to power. However, whereas Givers use this energy to help people, protectors use their energy in such a way that may actually scare others for their own benefit and sense of right and wrong. When a Giver moves to the positive side of the Protector, they can feel more confident, which allows them more honestly. They stop worrying so much about what other people think about them. When a Giver moves toward the negative side of the Protector, they lose their loving nature and turn irritable. They can isolate themselves and start making demands on other people. They might even become controlling towards other people.

Overlaps Between the Giver and Other Non-connected Types

Epicure 7: The Epicure is similar to the Giver because of their shared energetic attitudes. They are people pleasers who can even be seductive in their behaviors towards others. They differ because Epicures like to focus on themselves and what they want and can easily become self-absorbed. The Giver, instead, is always focused on other people and easy to sacrifice his or her sense of self.

Mediator 9: Givers and Mediators are both people pleasers who can lose their own sense of self in pursuit of feeling needed. Givers do this more actively, in search of approval, while Mediators do this reactively, as they are pulled between competing forces. Givers can be too intrusive, while Mediators are not intrusive at all.

Chapter 12: Enneagram For Relationships

We're social beings so if you're looking to find out what your Enneagram type is so that you can use the knowledge to start and build relationships, that's perfectly understandable. Because the Enneagram system has a realistic take on personality and how people interact, it emphasizes that there is no such thing as a doomed pairing, or one that is guaranteed to work.

The Enneagram merely provides an overview of how a person views and processes things, as well as the communication styles they use and prefer. That way, you can get some understanding on potential issues that may arise between you and another person.

All types can have fulfilling relationships with another type so long as both partners have self-awareness. Two persons with poor levels of self-awareness is a recipe for disaster. Even if one of you has high levels of self-awareness, it still wouldn't work because eventually, the two of you won't be able to understand each other.

Nonetheless, there are pairings that seem to appear more often, which is what a study by 9types seemed to confirm. However, keep in mind that there are also other factors at play, such as gender. For example, A Type 1 (Reformer) woman's most common match is a Type 9 man (Peacemaker) whereas a Type 1 man's common match is a Type 2 (Helper). Again, there is no guarantee that such a pairing is likely to be more successful – it's just certain types seem to be drawn to another type.

In addition, having the same type as your partner's does not guarantee success.

There is no magical pairing. However, there are fundamental aspects to relationship that should help you build yours, no matter who you are and who you're with. One of the biggest minds that contributed to Enneagram philosophy, David Daniels, mentioned the three:

1. Knowing What To Acknowledge

This is what you need to discover about yourself to find out what could cause distress to your partner and harm your relationship. A Type 1, for example, can be such a perfectionist which would be perfect if in an academic setting. However, if you constantly criticize your partner, you're likely going to end up damaging their self-esteem. So if you're a type 1, be careful with hurtful words and compliment your partner. Don't be too hard on them.

2. Knowing What To Appreciate

This aspect entails taking note of all the positive attributes about your partner that you need to acknowledge, and show support and appreciation for. For example, a type 3 (Achiever) is so competent but they don't really seek the spotlight and sometimes, they lose touch with their emotional core. Let them know you recognize the value of what they've accomplished or are trying to accomplish and go all out – be giddy about it.

3. Actions That Build The Relationship – This refers not just to the things you need to start doing but also to those that you need to stop doing. This involves showing appreciation, and gestures that resonate with a particular type.

In the following chapters, there is a dedicated section for relationships with a particular type.

The Point Nine Archetype: THE PEACEMAKER

The peacemaker believes that it's important to go with the flow and to blend in – that that's how they can find love and their own place in this world. That's why peacemakers tend to seek harmony.

Can't we all just get along? This is what a peacemaker typically has on his mind. They tend to be quite zen, but conflict stresses them out.

A peacemaker tends to focus on other people's agendas and their external environment. As a result, they tend to forget their own needs. They may end up caring too much about others that they forget to take care of themselves.

Nines are peace-loving people but this doesn't mean that they don't notice when they're being overlooked or taking advantage of. Being overlooked can become a deep source of sadness for people with this personality type.

Identifying A Peacemaker

Nines may have a hard time realizing they are the Peacemaker type because they tend to identify themselves with those who are closest to them. For example, they may identify themselves as a Helper especially if they have children. Peacemakers and Helpers are both considerate and likeable but whereas the former is self-effacing, the later know exactly how important they are.

Peacemakers also tend to be introverted where helpers are usually extroverted.

Dominant Traits

Peacemakers are:

Amiable – Nines are pretty easy to get along with. Others usually see them as warm, friendly, and peaceful. They're unpretentious so others tend to be at ease in their company.

Supportive. Nines are generally trusting and supportive as they often see the best in other people.

Caring - Nines have so much empathy and it shows. They make other people feel heard and understood.

Introverted - The dominant characteristics of Nines make them appear to be introverts – and to an extent, they are. They are rather reserved as they do not try to make themselves the center of everything. However, they do not exactly shun company. In fact, they thrive on having connection with others.

Optimistic. They tend to think that things will somehow work themselves out.

Tolerant – Other experience describe Nines as receptive and nonjudgmental.

People-pleasing – Not only would nines would go out of their way to cooperate; they also try to make sure that the group is working in harmony. However, they may appear to be indecisive because they don't want to rock the boat.

Adaptable – It's true that Nines do not like change. However, they're surprisingly able to cope when the changes do take effect.

Calming – Many nines also tend to be patient. They do things in a steady and sustainable way

Mindset

For a peacemaker, there is nothing in life that's better than being valued. That's why they are so focused on their environment. They're always on the lookout for things they feel they could contribute to.

Nines also have this uncanny ability to put themselves in other people's shoes. As a result, they can see the side to every issue which allows them to help people work things out.

They have a problem standing up for themselves at times. They have a hard time saying no when asked for something. However, they can become resentful if it was something they'd rather not do.

They prefer structured processes and like having established protocols because they want to know exactly how to deal with something the right way. That's why they develop pretty habits and their own procedures quickly.

They're not sure about what they really want and this is exacerbated by the fact that they focus too much on what other people want. They also rarely express what they really think and would try to subdue what they secretly tell themselves.

They dislike conflict so they'd rather do their best to maintain the status quo instead of rocking the boat. So, when it comes to relationships or problems in the workplace, they're, to an extent resigned – they'd silently accept some things that annoy or displease them.

This doesn't mean that they don't feel strong emotions. They do feel intense emotions such as anger but they try to appear easygoing (and they are!) and even tempered. They don't want to let themselves lose their cool. They'd rather pay attention to what other people have got going on. If you're having an awful day, expect nines to commiserate like it's their own misery, and if you're having a good day, you can expect them to celebrate with you like it's their own victory. That's why most people would see them as rather amiable.

Fears

Nines seek harmony so they tend to avoid conflict as much as they can, to the point that they can become too conciliatory and indecisive.

They hate change. They do not want being out of their comfort zone. They typically cannot cope well with separation. This is why they can be stubborn at times.

Nines appear introvert in their efforts to avoid exposing themselves to chaos. They withdraw a bit from life to protect themselves. Nonetheless, they can be social and active, although they can be rather reserved.

Core Desires

A Nine's ultimate desire is peace. They enjoy life's simple pleasures and would want nothing more than harmony. They are laid back and tend to make people around them feel safe and comfortable. They do not like confrontation or creating a scene.

What Nines Need To Work On

The ultimate goal of a peacemaker should be to 'reclaim himself. For too long, he has spent too much energy for other people, forgetting himself in the process. If you're a nine, it will benefit you in the long run to recognize your own needs and wake up to the fact that you matter too. Establish your priorities.

Challenges That Nines Usually Face

Nines tend to get distracted easily because they care too much about other people and their surroundings. At work, it's typical for delays to occur because they don't say no or get distracted with having to take care of their colleague's issues. This also occurs in their personal life. They tend to unknowingly put off their own goals in order to put other people first. It's not uncommon for them to even realize how deeply they want a particular thing.

Nines typically aren't attuned to their own feelings because they are so focused with blending in or making other people feel better. They often overlook their own dreams and desires.

Nines whose ability to cope is not fully developed will also find themselves incapable of motivating themselves to perform an action that can bring about significant change. This doesn't mean that they will outright refuse the change; they are too non-confrontational to do that. However, they are usually able to adapt quite well when the change does come.

They also struggle with low self-worth. Nines may have problems in the workplace in that they rarely fight for credit. In fact, they tend to not give themselves enough credit, and this attitude leads to other people not taking them seriously, or not noticing their contributions. Some Nines even get taken for granted. This doesn't mean that Nines aren't aware of this. In fact, this can cause Nines to silently seethe about the lack of recognition, which then erupts into fits of temper, albeit rarely. This can also manifest in passive-aggressiveness in the form of deliberately yet subtly delaying certain tasks.

Career Options For Peacemakers

Certain aspects of peacemakers' personality could make it difficult for them to perform upper management (CEO) duties. These include indecisiveness and reluctance to perform drastic measures.

However, they have characteristics that enable them to become great managers particularly those that require coordination, such as in Human Resource. They make great liaison officers or mediators. That characteristic, as well as their being quite popular with colleagues also make them good coordinators.

Because they tend to accept others without judgment, and it's in their nature to want to improve the lives of others, they can thrive as psychologists and therapists especially in marriage and family counselling.

Peacemakers And Relationships

Peacemakers want to feel connected not just to other people but the world in general.

This warmth makes them excellent friends. They genuinely always try to see the good in you. That's why they are also quite trusting.

They have no problem getting people to like them because they are not judgmental. They also make very good listeners because they always try to focus on other people. They won't try to assert their own opinions; they will just be there for you.

They make supportive, caring, and loving parents, thanks in part to their capacity to see the best in others. They're the types who believe that everything will work out in the end.

In the workplace, they're colleagues like working with them because they're easygoing. However, because Nines aren't demanding, they are often neglected and they may end up having more tasks to carry out because they don't say no.

If you're loved one is a nine or you're trying to manage one, ask them about themselves and give them time to think about what they really feel. More strategies on dealing with nine can be found below.

Interacting With Nines

Nines are easygoing but it can be difficult to truly know what they feel, mostly because they aren't even aware of it, or they just don't want to acknowledge it. There are some ways to deal with this, and to improve your relationship with a Nine.

Ask they about what they want and need. They are not attuned to their own needs so it will take some time before you get a real answer. It's not that they're going to lie – they're just not used to taking the time to address their needs. They might need help realizing what's important to them.

However, avoid coming on too strong. Don't rush them into an answer, or create too much pressure. This applies to everything in general. Nines would be more than happy to oblige but they can get resentful if they realize that they're being overlooked if not outright taken advantage of. Let them know you appreciate what they do.

Nines tend to be people pleasers so they hardly ever say no, even to their own detriment. If you care about a Nine and you sense that they're actually reluctant about something, just let them know outright that it's ok to say no. Help them realize that they also need to take care of themselves instead of focusing too much on other people's agenda.

Nines thrive on encouragement and support., which they also give so freely. So talk to them about their plan and priorities and support the steps they plan to take.

How To Be Your Best Self As A Nine

Be on the lookout for your distractions. This is where mindfulness could come on handy. Mindfulness is the practice of bringing your thoughts to your environment. It's true that Nines are already hyper aware of their surroundings, but this time, place yourself at the center. Bring your attention to what you know you should be focusing on, depending on your evaluation of your priorities.

Love yourself. You deserve to be happy. It's normal to want your loved ones to be happy but remember that you're not responsible for every other person's happiness. Take care of yourself.

Practice decision making. Recognize that sometimes, you really have to make a choice, and sometimes, the decisions can be hard. Set priorities and fight ambivalence. It's understandable to want to avoid conflict but remember that internal harmony is much more valuable than external peace.

Say no when what is being asked of you is something that you're uncomfortable with. Let other people know when you have too much on your plate. It's okay to acknowledge that.

Speak up about your own needs and wants. You have to right to ask for what you want.

Keep in mind that you can't please everybody, and more importantly, you don't need anyone's approval. The only person you're answerable to is yourself. So don't try to be that person who tries so hard to get everyone to like them. It's not worth your sanity and it's not possible.

You can't escape change and conflict. That's just the way things are. You don't have to face each one but if it's unavoidable, remember that you're stronger than you know. Nines tend to not give themselves enough credit and you'd be surprised to know how easy it is for you to overcome change and conflict.

Face problems head on even when you're stressed. Be wary of being in denial or trying to avoid the problem. It's difficult but you can try to find solace in meditation.

Chapter 13: Tools For Transformation

The Enneagram is an ancient tool of uncertain origin, said to be brought in by real genies somehow. Also called the Sufi numbers is like the chess board game and some other things of amazing design that have always been around. The Enneagram is an outline of the nine basic personality types, it shows the advantages and limitations of every intelligent being born in this planet. The outline of the nine personality types with a modern interpretation is as follows.

The Perfectionist. The number one is a much-disciplined person wants the best quality at any price. They make pretty good villain characters in movies because they are very unconcerned with human suffering, they are the perfect inquisitor.

The Server, also known as the helper or the saint. They are usually very service oriented people, helping everyone.

Sometimes they become intrusive manipulators that want others to do what they want because they feel it is the only right and good way to do it in the Universe. A classic is the beggar that yells at people.

The Chameleon, also known as the climber. This guy is nice and all gifted but his niceness is just apparent. You can see them changing before your eyes and turning against you as a crisis emerges. Nobody can usually believe that they are fake personalities, because they build a nice smile and an outlook of a good character while in reality, they are kind of divorced from their true feelings.

The extra sensitive is an artist like personality. Tends to depression and envy of what others have done with their lives. Some suicidal tendencies are possible, because he is aware of his own impulses at the same time that feels guilty about it. For others it may seem as if such a person exaggerates in her emotional concerns about other people's reactions.

The paranoid nerd. This guy is very intellectual but at the same time, he gets distracted. He sees logical connections in everything. He always wants to know the right explanation for the relevant phenomena that occur everywhere. He may get paranoid and build conspiracy theories and cure all remedies. He likes recognition for his brilliant mind and also wants to find a way to fit in the world he sees around as somehow frightening.

The devil's advocate. He can be a loyal follower or a bad seditious gossiper enemy. Inside he has a lot of tension that he relieves by finding the worst interpretation possible for others people's behavior and telling everyone what his twisted mind thinks. He assumes everybody else to be the worst except the one that he is loyal to. He may look like an unconcerned bastard, but he is a very dutiful hardworking and a masochistic character.

The maniac. This guy is peter pan, he never grows up. He is always an immature child. He yells and fights for things and items that he needs so badly that it is even scary. It could be food, videogames, a ticket for the theater, you name it. He is selfish and not too often concerned about sharing the goods evenly.

The tyrant dictator. He could also make a great boss or leader. He has a very powerful personality, always grounded in the bottom line. When he is unbalanced, he may act as a mafia chief, threatening everybody who doesn't accommodate to his desires. In the positive side, he could be a true hero and philanthropist.

The nine is the most unavailable person in the planet. A peacemaker kind of alienated unconscious person that lives in a perpetual quiet disconnection. He or she may go with you to a party, and then forget completely that you are there.

Sometimes they have awakenings like oh my but you have been here all this time!

The Enneagram is in reality a master tool for transformation used by group dynamics trainers to create transformational exercises, touching every aspect of the human shadow limitations pool, with the intention to overcome it. It creates the most tremendous breakthroughs in shadow master transformations and it has been a matter for every serious study.

Chapter 14: The Loyalist (Type 6)

Also known as the Loyal Skeptic or the Traditionalist

Fifteen Signs You're A Loyalist

You hang on to toxic friendships and situations longer than you should.

You are perceived - and quite rightly so - as a good trouble-shooter. This is because you are excellent at anticipating problems and devising appropriate solutions.

You can hold a lot of tension in the area around your diaphragm.

You worry a lot. Let's face it, there are so many things that can go wrong!

You are loyal to ideas and belief systems as well as to your friends and family members.

You can have trouble connecting with your own inner guidance system. This can cause you to lack confidence in your own judgment.

A sense of security is of the utmost importance to you and finding and holding on to this security is a driving force.

You tend to ask for advice from many different people before making a decision. As you mature, however, the amount of people upon whose opinion you rely may lessen.

You are contradictory in nature and your personality contains many opposites. This is because you tend to go back and forth between various different influences. To paraphrase Walt Whitman - you are large, you contain multitudes!

The people around you know that you are reliable and that they can depend on you. You are always there for them.

You appreciate order. It is important for you to have a firm structure in place, to have double-checked all your facts and to have a back-up plan.

Peace of mind can be elusive for you.

You can be suspicious of other people and authorities. You wait until the person or organization has proven themselves fully before giving them your trust.

You might have a tendency to act defiantly against whatever it is that you find threatening. In this instance, you may become a rebel and challenge authority.

You are responsible, hard-working and trustworthy. Those who are lucky enough to have your friendship know that you will always have their backs.

Did you say "that could be me" more than a few times? If so, read on. You could be a Loyalist!

The Loyalist Overview

As a typical Six, you crave security above all else. This is because you wrestle with a deep-rooted sense of anxiety which is at the core of your being, whether you are aware of it or not.

Type Six on The Enneagram tends to worry a lot. They have no problem imagining all sorts of scenarios, far-fetched or otherwise, in which everything goes wrong. They fear that there is nothing steady enough to hold on to, so they attempt to create such steadiness for themselves, often in personal relationships.

Their propensity to imagine every single possible disastrous outcome makes the Type Six an excellent trouble-shooter, and therefore very useful for others to have around. But this is not much of a comfort for the Loyalist, who struggles to find peace of mind with this constant focus on potential problems.

This can also have the effect of causing the Six to lack spontaneity. Because how can they possibly carry out an action without meticulous planning first? If they don't do this, won't everything collapse like a house of cards?

This is a lot of anxiety to live with. It also makes the Six more suspicious than the average person. You really have to prove yourself to win the Loyalist's trust. But once you succeed in doing so, you have a steadfast friend for life. Loyalty is a fantastic trait, but the Six would do well to make sure they are not staying loyal to someone or something long after it is time to move on from them.

The Six often has a complicated relationship with authority. On the one hand, their desire to have someone or something to believe in might cause them to give their control over to an external force. On the other hand, they also have the propensity to distrust and be suspicious of authority. How confusing! Sometimes a Six individual will lean further in one direction than the other. Sometimes, they might go back and forth between these two different attitudes.

The Loyalist also has two different strategies when it comes to coping with fear. One strategy is phobic, which will cause them to be compliant and cooperative. The other is counter-phobic, which means that the Six will take a defiant stand against anything they find threatening. Rebelliousness and aggression can be the hallmark here.

There have been countless noteworthy Loyalists. Here are a number of them: Sigmund Freud, Robert F. Kennedy, Malcolm X, Diana, Princess of Wales, U2's Bono, Julia Roberts, Ellen Degeneres, Spike Lee, Krishnamurti, Edgar Hoover, George H.W. Bush, J.R.R. Tolkein, Melissa Etheridge, Bruce Springsteen, Mike Tyson, Woody Allen, Sally Field, David Letterman, Newt Gingrich, Jay Leno, Katie Holmes, Benn Affleck, Tom Hanks, Mel Gibson, Diane Keaton, Mark Wahlberg, Dustin Hoffman, Oliver Stone, Michael Moore, John Grisham, Prince Harry, Robert F. Kennedy, Mark Twain and Richard Nixon.

The Loyalist Levels

Healthy

Trusting

This trust is for the self yet it also extends to others. The healthy Six has got the balance right, maintaining their independence while at the same time achieving a cooperative interdependence with others. They are able to collaborate with others and work together in harmony. When the Six learns to believe in herself, she can act with courage and positivity, making her a fabulous leader. She will also be richly self-expressive.

Appealing to Others

When the Six is fully mature and gets her or himself together, they can be a most endearing and lovable type. People react strongly to them in a very positive way and have a genuine affection for them, which they are likely to receive back in kind. Once they have their trust issues sorted out, the healthy Six successfully blends with others, leading to fruitful friendships and alliances.

Dedicated

When the healthy Loyalist finds a movement or an individual in which they fully believe, there is no one who is more dedicated. They will build communities, sacrifice for others or for a greater cause, and bring cooperation, security and stability wherever they go. They are determined, reliable, trustworthy and responsible.

Neutral

Safe

At this neutral level, a kind of contraction occurs and the Loyalist has more of a tendency to play it safe. This is not always a terrible thing. At this point of their development, the Six invests their energy in whatever seems likely to remain stable and secure. They organize and create structure and look to authorities that can promise a sense of continuity. They never let up in anticipating what can go wrong and trying to put systems in place to prevent such problems occurring.

Indecisive

If the Six in neutral mode feels confused or that too many demands are being made on him or her, they will give off many contradictory signals. They will procrastinate and become overly cautious, indecisive and evasive. They will be increasingly negative as their anxiety levels rise and unpredictability results. They may even react in passive-aggressive ways.

Reactive

The fear takes over the Six, although they may not consciously be aware of this. Instead, they blame other people for their uncomfortable feelings, taking it out on the "outsider," for instance. They will be defensive at this level and highly sensitive to threats, constantly monitoring others to work out whether they are a friend or foe. They can be authoritarian and suspicious of everyone and their manner can become belligerent.

Unhealthy

Panicked

Fear takes over at this unhealthy stage. This highly insecure feeling causes the Six to panic and become extremely volatile. They look for increasingly strong authority figures and institutions in order to buoy up their own acute feelings of inferiority and defenselessness. They will be extremely critical and difficult to be around.

Persecuted

This all-pervasive feeling that others are out to get them can make the unhealthy Six lash out irrationally which, in the worst case scenario, can lead to violence.

Hysterical

This is the lowest a Six can go. It is a self-destructive level where alcohol and drugs might be abused. It is the realm of the Paranoid Personality Disorders and they might even attempt to take their own lives.

The Loyalist Wings

Type Six with a Five wing (6W5)

For the most part, the Type Six with a Five wing is a traditional sort, conservative in their views and desirous of fitting into a trustworthy group. Safety is the name of the game here. Although the Six desire to feel secure is colored by the Five need to analyze things right down to their component parts.

When well-balanced, the 6W5 is able to let go of anxiety. This makes them good-humored, relaxed and endearing. They finally feel that they can trust life and in turn, this is a person that can be trusted and relied upon one-hundred-percent.

It is lovely to have the balanced Type Six with a Five wing as a family member. Possessing a quiet confidence, they will be a wonderful companion and source of wisdom. You will be able to develop a deep bond with this type and the Five wing will add a perceptiveness to their enduring friendship.

But imbalance can sometimes ensue and anxiety can rear its ugly head again. They look for a reason for this rising tension and if one is not easily forthcoming, they will find someone to blame for it!

If stress levels increase, the world becomes an increasingly threatening place for the 6W5 and paranoia can begin to set in. They might feel that everybody is out to get them and in this desperately uncomfortable place of tension, they might look for somebody to come to their rescue.

Sixes want to be likable and attractive to others, but Five does not really know how to achieve this. Their attire tends not to be overly showy or flashy.

It may suit the Loyalist with a Five wing to find employment that combines being part of a group with being alone. A forest ranger or a bus driver might be an example of this. Some become involved in risky protection activities such as fire-fighting and others might look for ways to advocate for under privileged people.

The Type Six with a Seven wing (6W7)

The Type Six with a Seven wing is a lot less subdued than the Type Six with a Five wing. Their reactions are more impulsive and colourful and they are less likely to analyze a situation, instead jumping in with both feet. However, the caution of the Six will usually pull back the flamboyance of the Seven before it gets too out-of-hand.

There is a back and forth here between flamboyance and caution which can cause some emotional volatility.

At its best, the Loyalist with a Seven wing is steady, calm and deliberate. When in balance, both the Six's anxiety and the Seven's impulsiveness tend to diminish. They still love having fun with their friends but the desperate drive for security is transformed into an inner strength. They make great parents or siblings.

The 6W7 frequently develops a strong spiritual side, experiencing a deep sense of belonging with the universe. Their faith is a great source of comfort to them.

Of course, things can get out of kilter. If the Type Six with a Seven wing gets out of whack, anxiety and insecurity come to the fore once more. Here, they will jump from one extreme emotional state to the other, desperately searching for someone to help them and feeling increasing despair.

In a more stressed state, the 6W7 can come across as clingy and desperate and this drives other people away. They get themselves into all sorts of trouble as they feel increasingly dependent and tense.

This variant of the Six is often physically attractive and appealing to the opposite sex. In terms of the world of work, they may look to fun professions which also have an element of security inherent in them such as cartoonists or movie reviewers.

Advice for The Loyalist

Trust is an issue for you. If you are honest with yourself, you can most probably identify a few people in your life that you can trust completely. Cherish these people and hold them dear. Let them know how much you appreciate them, even though this might make you feel vulnerable. If you genuinely do not have anyone in your life that you feel you can trust, make it a point to find someone, believing that there are trustworthy people out there. You may have to move past your fears to do so, but the end result will be worth it.

The Type Six can sometimes use projection as a defense mechanism, in other words, attributing to others what you cannot accept in yourself. This hardly seems fair, does it? Watch out for your tendency to resort to this behaviour. Do not blame others for things that you yourself have done or brought upon yourself in some way. You become your own worst enemy when you become negative and self-doubting, causing even more harm to yourself than you do to others.

Do all you can to quell your anxiety. A key step might be to just accept that this is part of your nature and also to acknowledge that more people suffer from anxiety than you probably realize. Try to relax. Everything is going to be fine!

Other people like you more than you think they do. That's something else to stop worrying about!

Try not to overreact when you are under stress. This involves managing your own thoughts more effectively and acknowledging that most of what you have wasted your time worrying about has never arisen. Fearful thoughts have no purpose but to weaken your ability to act and make things better.

Conclusion

I must admit it's been quite a journey since the beginning of this book and I also commend your patience so far. However, it is still important to know that as entertaining as learning about personalities are, Enneagram goes beyond pure entertainment, the goal is to make relating easier and also, to give a deeper insight of understanding to a person about his or her strengths, weaknesses, preferences and attitude toward certain things.

The way you relate with people has a whole lot to do with understanding yourself and your personality which is definitely a major focus of the Enneagram as discussed in this book. Knowledge of your personality through the Enneagram is a revelation of yourself and that revelation will go a long way in helping you live a life of bliss, harmony, and help you live in a peaceful environment.

When you take the extra step of learning about others around you, you take a step towards developing and embracing a better relationship with everyone around you. It is no mystery that, when a cordial relationship is developed, you can be rest assured that you can live without holding grudges against anyone. Now it's up to you to put all the knowledge you've gained to good use and give the universe no other choice than to reward you by giving you peace. Turn obstacles to building blocks, build relationships with ease and most importantly, know who you are. Now, go out there and make a difference.

Thank you and God Bless!